Zion's Story

A Study and Meditation on What the Bible Has to Say about Eternity

Skip Copeland

Copyright © 2023 Skip Copeland

All rights reserved.

ISBN: 979-8858662938

IN MEMORY OF KRIS

All the promises of God find their Yes in Christ, whom
Heaven must receive until the time for
restoring all the things which God spoke about by the
mouth of his holy prophets long ago.

For the LORD has chosen Zion;
he has desired it for his dwelling place:
"This is my resting place forever;
here I will dwell, for I have desired it."

And the ransomed of the LORD shall return
and come to Zion with singing;
everlasting joy shall be upon their heads;
they shall obtain gladness and joy
and sorrow and sighing shall flee away.

Zion's Story

CONTENTS

	Preface	i
1	The Story Begins	1
2	God In the Midst of His People	9
3	The Mountain of God	25
4	To Dwell Forever in Zion	35
5	The Return to Zion	57
6	Zion – The End Game	79
7	Epilogue	93
	Abbreviations	125
	Bibliography	126
	Scripture Index	127

PREFACE

Scholars dispute and debate the origins of "Zion theology" in the Old Testament. But by the time of the Babylonian exile, the grip of Zion's story on those in exile was palpable. Even their captors were aware of the importance of Zion to the exiles. Psa 137:1-6 records the mournful lament of the exiles over their plight:

> ¹*By the waters of Babylon,*
>   *there we sat down and wept,*
>   *when we remembered Zion.*
> ²*On the willows there*
>   *we hung up our lyres.*
> ³*For there our captors*
>   *required of us songs,*
>   *and our tormentors, mirth, saying,*
>   *"Sing us one of the songs of Zion!"*
> ⁴*How shall we sing the* LORD*'s song*
>   *in a foreign land?*
> ⁵ *If I forget you, O Jerusalem,*
>   *let my right hand forget its skill!*
> ⁶*Let my tongue stick to the roof of my mouth,*
>   *if I do not remember you,*
>   *if I do not set Jerusalem*
>   *above my highest joy!*

What was it about Zion that created such emotion, and does the story of Zion have any meaning or relevance for Christians today?

I have read more than a dozen books on "Zion theology," and perused (in the *primary* dictionary sense of the word) several modern "scholarly" commentaries on the Psalms and the Prophets seeking wisdom and understanding on what the Old Testament has to say about "Zion." I could tell you about the different "theories" regarding the origin of Zion and their principal themes and motifs, and maybe impress one or two of you of my erudite mastery of the subject. But all I learned from all that reading was just how *much* the Old Testament has to say about Zion. Very little of what I read helped me to put it all together in a cogent and meaningful way. That happened – understanding and insight – only by immersing myself in the words of scripture themselves, sorting them out with the help of a few "hermeneutic keys." For those unfamiliar with the expression, a hermeneutic key is a compelling insight from one (or more) passages that helps make sense of other passages that seem difficult or obscure. In the final chapter I summarize some of the hermeneutic keys that led me to my understanding of Zion's story.

To focus on the Bible's own words, I have studiously avoided citing human sources except for occasional lexical references that I think provide insight into the meaning of the words being used to tell the story of Zion. And for the same reason, I have copiously quoted scripture. When I started out, it was my hope that I might, in the end, have more words of scripture in this study than words of my own. I did not get there, but if you ignore this preface, the footnotes, and the epilogue, the main body of text in chapters 1-6 is nearly half (45%) scripture. I would hope that the reader will take their time, reading the quoted words of scripture slowly and carefully, certainly reflecting and even meditating on them. You will find that Zion's story tells of a glorious future for God's children that is unlike what most believe awaits them in eternity. While spending eternity in Heaven with God would be glorious, the glory that God has prepared for us in Zion is far greater, a sentiment expressed by Psa 87:1-3:

> [1]*On the holy mount stands the city he founded;*
> [2]*the LORD loves the gates of Zion*
> *more than all the dwelling places of Jacob.*
> [3]*Glorious things of you are spoken,*
> *O city of God.*

It will be the best of *both* worlds, having all the glory of Heaven, because the LORD will be there, and having all the glory of this world as God intended for it in the beginning, Gen 1:1, 31a:

> [1]*In the beginning, God created the heavens and the earth...*[31a]*And God saw everything that he had made, and behold, it was very good.*

You will find some style peculiarities in my writing. Heaven, with a capital "H," is the "highest heaven" where God (for now) reigns on His throne over all creation. Throughout this book, I use "God," "LORD" (all caps) and "Yahweh" interchangeably. While in New Testament contexts "God" refers to the "Father," in Old Testament contexts the three terms refer to what we know from the New Testament as the "Trinity." There is no necessary "rhyme or reason" to my choice of which to use when referring to Yahweh in the Old Testament. Sometimes I am following the lead of a passage of scripture under consideration. At other times I am just mixing things up because each is an honorable and meaningful way to refer to the Creator.

This is not a long book. You can skip the footnotes and epilogue and read the main body of the text in less than two hours (at what is considered an average rate of speed for reading). And you do not need to read the footnotes or epilogue to adequately understand the basics of Zion's story. But I subtitled the book *"A Study and Meditation on What the Bible Has to Say about Eternity"* for a reason. In my experience, even Christians who systematically read through the Bible are surprised when I point out some of the things that are revealed in the Old Testament. Most are clueless about the "hermeneutic keys" I discuss in the epilogue.

Obviously, just *reading* scripture is not enough. We bring a lot of preconceptions to our reading of scripture, tending to create "confirmation bias." As a result, we can read certain texts over and over, and never realize that what is being said fundamentally challenges some strongly held belief previously assumed as fact. Only *careful* and *open-minded* study and reflection can overcome such bias. Prayer can help, also. I pray that this book will help you better understand the glory that is to be revealed to us when the LORD's plan for the fulness of time at last comes to pass.

I would be remiss not to mention the assistance I received from several who read a major draft of Zion's Story. While the overall review I received from them was supportive, there was also some significant, but always constructive, criticism or concerns expressed regarding my take on certain matters. While this did not lead to any significant revision in how I read what scripture has to say about Zion's Story, it did lead to numerous edits to clarify, and better nuance, what I think about the matters under discussion. In a couple of instances, I chose to address some of these concerns in footnotes, rather than get sidetracked with discussing them in the basic storyline. I trust that those who read Zion's Story in draft will see where and how they have influenced the final version. They certainly made the final version better than the draft that I gave them. But of course, I must take responsibility for any remaining faults or failings.

And finally, this book would not be were it not for the word of God. In scripture we find "words of life," words about the hope of God's people for life now and in the age to come. In scripture we find Zion's story. It is a story about how much the LORD loves His creation, including the earth, which He created to be inhabited forever by the crowning glory of His creation, humanity. If Zion's story teaches anything, it teaches that an eternity without an earth inhabited by all of God's creatures is unthinkable. Only when the *earth* is filled with the glory of the LORD, as the waters cover the sea, will God's eternal purpose finally be fulfilled.

1 THE STORY BEGINS

The story of "Zion" in scripture begins long before David's conquest (c. 1010 BC) of the Jebusite stronghold, 1 Chr 11:4-9, and his bringing the Ark to Jerusalem, 2 Sam 6:12-15. The story is at least as old as "the Song of the Sea" celebrating Yahweh's victory over Pharoah and the deliverance of the Israelites from Egyptian bondage recorded in Exod 15:1-18.[1] In vv. 16-18 the Song concludes:

> [16]*Terror and dread fall upon them; because of the greatness of your arm, they are still as a stone, till* **your people**, *O* L<small>ORD</small>, *pass by, till* **the people** *pass by whom you have purchased.*[2]

---

[1] The date of the Exodus is the source of much controversy. A literal reading of 1 Kgs 6:1 would suggest a mid-15th century BC date, e.g., c. 1450 BC. Others argue for a later, 13th century BC date, relying on archaeological evidence. But the later date does not appear to allow enough time for the period of the Judges.

[2] The "purchase" motif is a synonym for the Exodus as a story of "redemption" and is explicitly tied to "Mount Zion" in Psa 74:2. While Israel's Exodus serves as an example of God redeeming His people, the true and final story of redemption postdates the Old Testament period, Mal 3:17, 1 Pet 2:9.

> ¹⁷*You will bring them in and plant them **on your own mountain, the place**, O LORD, which you have made **for your abode, the sanctuary**, O Lord, which your hands have established.*
> ¹⁸*The LORD will reign **forever and ever**.*[3]

The terror and dread of v. 16 is what befell the nations that Israel "passed by" on its journey to the promised land (cf. what Rahab said in Josh 2:8-11). The "mountain" of v. 17, which God will take for his "abode, the sanctuary," is Zion, the "mountain of the LORD of hosts," Psa 48:1-3, 87:1-2, 99:9.

Forty years later, after the punishing journey of wilderness wanderings, Moses revisits this promise in Deut 12:5-7:

> ⁵*But you shall seek **the place** that the LORD your God will choose out of all your **tribes to put his name and make his habitation there**. There you shall go, ⁶and there you shall bring your burnt offerings and your sacrifices, your tithes and the contribution that you present, your vow offerings, your freewill offerings, and the firstborn of your herd and of your flock. ⁷And there you shall eat before the LORD your God, and you shall rejoice, you and your households, in all that you undertake, in which the LORD your God has blessed you.*

While for a time Sinai was known as "the mountain of God," Exod 3:1, 4:27, 24:13, after the Ark was settled in Zion and the glory of the LORD filled the Temple, 1 Kgs 8:1-11, Zion replaced Sinai as "the mountain of God."

This transition from Sinai to Zion (Jerusalem), and

---

[3] Scripture quotations are from the ESV, unless otherwise noted.

Zion's Story

Zion's place in Yahweh's plan for humanity, was celebrated in Psalm 68, vv. 7-8, 15-17, 24, 29, 35:

> ⁷**O God, when you went out before your people,**
>   **when you marched through the wilderness,** Selah
> ⁸the earth quaked, the heavens poured down rain,
>   before God, the One of Sinai, before God, the God of Israel.
> ¹⁵O mountain of God, mountain of Bashan; O many-peaked mountain, mountain of Bashan!
> ¹⁶Why do you look with hatred, O many-peaked mountain, at **the mount that God desired for his abode, yes, where the L**ORD **will dwell forever**?
> ¹⁷The chariots of God are twice ten thousand, thousands upon thousands; the LORD is among them;
>   **Sinai is now in the sanctuary.**
> ²⁴Your procession is seen, O God, the procession of my God, my King, **into the sanctuary—**
> ²⁹Because of your **temple at Jerusalem**
>   kings shall bear gifts to you.
> ³²O kingdoms of the earth, sing to God;
>   sing praises to the LORD, Selah
> ³³to him who rides in the heavens, the ancient heavens;
>   behold, he sends out his voice, his mighty voice.
> ³⁴Ascribe power to God, whose majesty is over Israel,
>   and whose power is in the skies.
> ³⁵**Awesome is God from his sanctuary**; the God of Israel—
>   he is the one who gives power and strength
>   to his people. Blessed be God!

Like Exodus 15 and Deuteronomy 12, the beginning of Zion's story is traced back to the period of wilderness wanderings. Verses 15-16 mock the Canaanite Baal religion as being jealous that Yahweh passed up establishing His sanctuary on Mt. Hermon, a mountain central to Baal worship, as the Israelites passed through Bashan (modern day Golan Heights) defeating King Og, Num 21:33-35, on their way out of the wilderness and into Canaan. Zion's story would continue until the LORD came to dwell on "the mount" (v.16) in the temple at Jerusalem (v.29). Sinai, which had previously been "the mountain of God," was now said to be "in the sanctuary," v.17.

Zion was to be *the place on earth* where God was to dwell forever (v. 16), the place where God would "make His name to dwell" (Deut 12:5, 11, 14:23, 16:2, 6, 11)[4] and where He would dwell in the midst of all creation (cf. Gen 3:8, discussed more fully in Chapter 2, pp. 20-22), but especially in the midst of "His people" (v. 35). The language of the place where God would "put His name" or "make His name to dwell" are figures of speech for asserting both ownership *and* residence, a place where people would go be in the presence of the LORD in order to invoke His name and petition for divine blessings. While Yahweh

---

[4] There is dispute over whether these verses refer to a *sole* "place" where God was to be worshiped, or merely the *central* place of worship. From John 4:20-21 it seems clear that there was a sense that wherever the sanctuary (temple) was, it was not just a central place of worship but *the* place where Yahweh would "dwell." For a time, this "place" was Shiloh, Josh 18:1, cf. 1 Sam 1:3, Jer 7:12. But from 1 Kgs 8:16, 29, and especially 1 Kgs 9:3 ("I have consecrated this house that you have built, by putting my name there *forever*. My eyes and my heart will be there *for all time*.") we see there is some sense in which Zion/Jerusalem was to be *the* place where God would dwell *forever*. This does not contradict what Jesus says in John 4:21-24. In John's vision of the new Jerusalem in Revelation 21-22, the whole (new) earth becomes the throne of God and fills the (new) earth with God's glory (cf. Rev 21:10-11, 22:1, 3-5, such that the glory of the LORD at last fills "all the earth," Num 14:21, Psa 72:19, Isa 11:9, Hab 2:14.

dwelt *literally* in the sanctuary (the "Most Holy" place of the Tabernacle, and then later the Temple) as the "Shekinah glory"[5] (a visible manifestation of the Divine Presence), Zion came eventually to represent the entire city of Jerusalem, and not just the inner sanctuary. Or perhaps we should say that the name of the city came to be associated with Zion as the place where Yahweh dwelt in the midst His people.[6]

But Zion and Jerusalem were more than just geographical place-names. Besides the obvious import of the city being the "place" where Yahweh would make His name known, and the place of His habitation, it was a city associated with the people of God, Isa 51:16:

> [16]*And I have put my words in your mouth
> and covered you in the shadow of my hand,
> establishing* **the heavens**
> *and laying* **the foundations of the earth,**
> *and saying to Zion,* **'You are my people.'"**

It is notable that Zion is here associated with creation itself, the establishment of the heavens and the laying of the foundations of the earth, Gen 1:1. Few things, if any, are more associated with the power and might, the majesty and glory, and the benevolence of God than His creation of the heavens and the earth. Moreover, if the LORD

---

[5] "Shekinah" is not a biblical word per se. It was coined by the Rabbis to refer to the "Divine Presence" of Yahweh dwelling in the Most Holy Place, and is etymologically related to *šāḵan* (verb, to dwell, or tabernacle, Strong's #H7931) and *miškān* (noun, dwelling, or tabernacle, Strong's #H4908).

[6] For examples of the close association of Zion with the city of Jerusalem, see Psa 51:18, 102:21, 128:5, 135:21, 147:2, Isa 4:3-4, 10:12, 24:23, 30:19, 52:1-2, Amos 1:2, Mic 4:2, Joel 2:32, 3:16-17, Zeph 3:14, 16, Zech 1:14, 17, 8:3, 8.

was to dwell in Zion *forever*, Psa 68:15-16, then as the center of God's creation, all of creation itself, the heavens and the earth, would have to last forever. We will consider this point more thoroughly in chapter 4 (pp. 46-55).

Though later desecrated by the unfaithfulness of Judah and left desolate in the wake of Babylonian destruction, Yahweh sees a future for Jerusalem for those who repent, so that it would come to be known a city of righteousness, a city of "The Holy People, The Redeemed of the Lord:"

Isa 1:25-27
> ²⁵*I will turn my hand against you*
> *and will smelt away your dross as with lye*
> *and remove all your alloy.*
> ²⁶*And I will restore your judges as at the first,*
> *and your counselors as at the beginning.*
> *Afterward you shall be called*
> ***the city of righteousness, the faithful city."***
> ²⁷***Zion*** *shall be redeemed by justice,*
> *and those in her who repent, by righteousness.*

Isa 60:14
> ¹⁴*The sons of those who afflicted you shall come bending low to you, and all who despised you shall bow down at your feet; they shall call* **you the City of the Lord, the Zion of the Holy One of Israel.**

Isa 62:11-12
> ¹¹*Behold, the Lord has proclaimed*
> *to the end of the earth:*
> *Say to Daughter **Zion**,*⁷
> *"Behold, your salvation comes;*

---

⁷ The ESV's "Say to the daughter of Zion" has been changed to follow the NET Bible and other translations which reflect recent lexical scholarship that the Hebrew here, *baṯ ṣîyôn*, refers not to any particular citizens of Zion, but to Zion itself as the daughter of the Lord. See NIDOTTE, 1:780, 6.

> behold, his reward is with him,
> and his recompense before him."
> ¹²And **they shall be called The Holy People,**
> **The Redeemed of the** LORD;
> and **you shall be called Sought Out,**
> **A City Not Forsaken.**

Attesting further to Zion as the place where Yahweh dwells with a righteous remnant of His people are the frequent references to Zion as His "holy hill," Psa 2:6, 3:4, 15:1, 43:3, Jer 31:23, Dan 9:16, 20.

Summing up what we have learned so far, when God brought His people out of the land of Egypt and into the Promised Land, He was guiding them to a *place* where He would "make His name to dwell," a *city*, where He was to "dwell forever," and which was to be peopled by *His* people, known for their *righteousness*. Geographically this city was known as Zion or Jerusalem, but other epithets were often applied to it, such as *the city of righteousness, the faithful city,* and the LORD's *holy hill.* Later, in prophecy, she would be known as *the Redeemed of the* LORD, and *Sought Out, A City Not Forsaken.*

These later epithets beg a question we will put off for now, which is *when* would Zion become known as *the Redeemed of the* LORD and *Sought Out, A City Not Forsaken?"* Closely related to understanding Zion as a "city of righteousness" *in the future* is that it was a place where Yahweh would dwell "in the midst" of His people. To understand what that means is the focus of the next chapter.

Zion's Story

2 GOD IN THE MIDST OF HIS PEOPLE

Numerous Old Testament texts describe Zion as the place where the LORD would dwell "in the midst" of His people:

Isa 12:3-6
> ^{3}With joy you will draw water from the wells of salvation. ^{4}And you will say **in that day**:
>>   "Give thanks to the LORD,
>>   call upon his name,
>>   make known his deeds among the peoples,
>>   proclaim that his name is exalted.
>> ^{5}"Sing praises to the LORD, for he has done gloriously;
>>   let this be made known in all the earth.
>> ^{6}Shout, and sing for joy, **O inhabitant of Zion**,
>>   for great **in your midst** is the Holy One of Israel."

Psa 46:4-5
> ^{4}There is a river whose streams make glad the city of God,
>   the holy habitation of the Most High.
> ^{5}God **is in the midst of her**; she shall not be moved;
>   God will help her when morning dawns.

Ezek 43:7a, 9
> ^{7a}and he said to me, "Son of man, this is **the place of**

my throne and the place of the soles of my feet, where I will dwell in the midst of the people of Israel forever.
⁹*Now let them put away their whoring and the dead bodies of their kings far from me, and **I will dwell in their midst forever.***

Hos 11:9

⁹*I will not execute my burning anger;*
  I will not again destroy Ephraim;
for I am God and not a man,
  the Holy One in your midst,
and I will not come in wrath.

Joel 2:23, 26-27

²³*"Be glad, **O children of Zion**,*
  and rejoice in the LORD *your God,*
for he has given the early rain for your vindication;
  he has poured down for you abundant rain,
the early and the latter rain, as before.
²⁶*"You shall eat in plenty and be satisfied,*
  and praise the name of the LORD *your God,*
who has dealt wondrously with you.
  And my people shall never again be put to shame.
²⁷*You shall know that I am **in the midst of Israel**,*
  and that I am the LORD *your God and there is none else.*
And my people shall never again be put to shame.

Zeph 3:15-17

¹⁵*The* LORD *has taken away the judgments against you;*
  he has cleared away your enemies.
The King of Israel, the LORD, ***is in your midst**;*
  you shall never again fear evil.
¹⁶***On that day** it shall be said to Jerusalem:*
  *"Fear not, **O Zion**;*
let not your hands grow weak.
¹⁷*The* LORD *your God **is in your midst**,*
  a mighty one who will save;

Zion's Story

> *he will rejoice over you with gladness;*
> *he will quiet you by his love;*
> *he will exult over you with loud singing.*

Zech 2:5, 10-11

> ⁵*And I will be to her a wall of fire all around, declares the* L<small>ORD</small>, *and **I will be the glory in her midst**.*
>
> ¹⁰*Sing and rejoice, **Zion** my daughter!*[8] *for behold, **I come and I will dwell in your midst**, declares the* L<small>ORD</small>. ¹¹*And many nations shall join themselves to the* L<small>ORD</small> *in that day, and **shall be my people**. And **I will dwell in your midst**, and you shall know that the* L<small>ORD</small> *of hosts has sent me to you.* ¹² *And the* L<small>ORD</small> *will inherit Judah as his portion **in the holy land**, and will **again choose Jerusalem**."*

Zech 8:3, 7-8

> ³*Thus says the* L<small>ORD</small>: *I have returned to **Zion** and **will dwell in the midst of Jerusalem**, and Jerusalem shall be called **the faithful city**, and **the mountain of the*** L<small>ORD</small> ***of hosts, the holy mountain**.*
>
> ⁷*Thus says the* L<small>ORD</small> *of hosts: Behold, I will save my people from the east country and from the west country,* ⁸*and **I will bring them to dwell in the midst of Jerusalem**. And they shall be my people, and I will be their God, in faithfulness and in righteousness."*

The importance of properly understanding the theological sense of the expression "in the midst" cannot be over-

---

[8] Following the NET Bible, I have replaced the ESV's "O daughter of Zion" with the NET Bible's "Zion my daughter." The note accompanying this reading in the NET Bible explains: "This individualizing of Zion as a *daughter* draws attention to the corporate nature of the covenant community and also to the tenderness with which the L<small>ORD</small> regards his chosen people." Cf. footnote 7.

stated. But before we pursue this further, some observations about the preceding texts are in order.

The prophetic texts (e.g., all but the text from Psalm 46) are, well, *prophetic*, i.e., describing something that will take place in Israel's future. We will see below (p. 18) that this "future" being described belongs not to physical Israel, but to spiritual Israel. In other words, the texts have relevance for us *today* and are telling us something about *our future*. For example, Isa 12:3-6, with its "in that day" is clearly messianic. The reading from Joel 2 directly precedes Joel 2:28-29 cited by the Apostle Peter in Acts 2 on the Day of Pentecost. The reading from Ezekiel 43 is part of Ezekiel's vision of an eschatological end-time temple with strong parallels to Revelation 21-22. Even Psalm 46, while not strictly prophecy, is nevertheless depicting Zion as an *ideal* and would thus be descriptive of the Zion *yet to come*. So, all of what is cited above speaks to us *today* and demands careful and serious consideration as to what it means for our own *future destiny*.

For example, as noted, Ezekiel's vision of an end-time eschatological temple shares strong affinities with Revelation 21-22. Yes, there are stark differences and things about Ezekiel's vision that we cannot take literally.[9] It should be of no real concern when two different *figura-*

---

[9] The most obvious example of this would be the practice of animal sacrifice in Ezekiel's vision. And the obvious explanation is that even as the sacrifice of the original temple (and tabernacle) was never more than a *type* of the perfect sacrifice to come, so the sacrifice in Ezekiel's vision of an eschatological end-time temple is simply a figure for the sacrifice that will accompany the real end-time temple, i.e., the atoning sacrifice of Jesus Christ.

tive or *metaphorical* word pictures do not exactly or literally line up together. The river that flows from the temple in Ezekiel 47 has trees on both sides, with "leaves for healing," 47:12, like Rev 22:2. But the river in Ezekiel's vision is full of fish, and fishermen cast their nets into it; there is nothing like this in Revelation 22. Such disparate visions can be describing the same thing even though the figures in the visions diverge dramatically. It is what stands *behind* the imagery that matters when seeking to interpret or understand figurative Biblical language.[10]

With that in mind, what might we take away from the description of Ezekiel's temple in Ezek 43:7a? Repeating:

> [7a]*and he said to me, "Son of man, this is* **the place of my throne and the place of the soles of my feet,** *where I will dwell in the midst of the people of Israel forever.*

Note first what is said about this new temple being "the place of my throne." Until now (the eschatological future being described in Ezekiel's vision) God's throne has always been depicted as being in Heaven:

Isa 66:1-2a
> [1]*Thus says the* LORD:
>   *"***Heaven is my throne,**
>   *and* **the earth is my footstool;**
>   *what is the house that you would build for me,*
>   *and what is the place of my rest?*
> [2]*All these things my hand has made,*

---

[10] Some who read a draft of Zion's Story expressed concern over the decision as to when to treat something as figurative or literal might appear arbitrary to some. The basis for treating some aspects of Old Testament prophecy as literal and other as figurative is not arbitrary, but is based upon scripture. Cf. footnote 12, and again, more fully, in the final chapter, at footnote 74).

and so all these things came to be,
declares the LORD.

Psa 11:4
⁴*The LORD is in his holy temple;* **the LORD's throne is in heaven;** *his eyes see, his eyelids test the children of man.*

Psa 103:19
¹⁹*The LORD has established* **his throne in the heavens,** *and his kingdom rules over all.*

Whereas the LORD is normally depicted as being on His throne *in Heaven*, here His throne is depicted as being *on earth,* in the eschatological new Temple. Nor is this the only place where the LORD's throne in the future is depicted as being on to earth. Consider Jer 3:17:

¹⁷*At that time Jerusalem shall be called the throne of the LORD, and all nations shall gather to it, to the presence of the LORD in Jerusalem, and they shall no more stubbornly follow their own evil heart.*

Now all of Jerusalem, all of Zion, has become "the throne of the LORD." What accounts for this change, that the throne of the LORD is also now *on earth*?

While we will consider Revelation 21-22 more fully later, we cannot help here but to note that Revelation 21-22 depicts the same thing, the throne of God *on earth*.[11]

---

[11] Some point out that Rev 21:2 does not say that the new Jerusalem came down "out of Heaven *to earth*." That the words "to earth" are not explicitly found in the text is neither grammatically nor exegetically compelling. When Jesus said, in John 6:38, "For I have come down from heaven," he did not need add "to earth" for us to understand what he was saying. Both here, and in John 6:38, the context makes it clear what is being said. In Revelation 21-22, the vision is not taking place *in Heaven*. In 21:10 John is carried in

In the opening verses of Revelation 21, a "new Jerusalem" is seen coming down "out of Heaven" to a *new earth*. And in the opening verses of chapter 22, vv. 1-5, we find *God enthroned* in the new Jerusalem, new Zion:

> ¹*Then the angel showed me the river of the water of life, bright as crystal, flowing from* **the throne of God** *and of the Lamb* ²*through the middle of the* **street of the city**; *also, on either side of the river, the tree of life with its twelve kinds of fruit, yielding its fruit each month. The leaves of the tree were for the healing of the nations.* ³*No longer will there be anything accursed,* **but the throne of God** *and of the Lamb* **will be in it***, and his servants will worship him.* ⁴*They will see his face, and his name will be on their foreheads.* ⁵*And night will be no more. They will need no light of lamp or sun, for the Lord God will be their light, and they will reign forever and ever.*

Both visions, the Old Testament vision of Ezekiel, and the New Testament vision of the Apostle John, see the throne of God *now on earth* (in the age to come).

Equally significant is what the LORD says to Ezekiel about how the place of the new Temple on earth will be "the place of the soles of my feet." Recall how in Isa 66:1 the LORD describes *the earth* as His "footstool." During the time in which the Shekinah Glory inhabited the Most Holy Place of the Tabernacle and Temple, the Ark of the Covenant was considered the "footstool" of God on

---

the spirit to a *high mountain* to watch the descent of the new Jerusalem, an obvious intertextual allusion to Ezek 40:2. Though a vision, John is watching the descent of the new Jerusalem from a vantage-point *on earth* (just as Ezekiel did), as it comes down out of Heaven *to earth*. A *new* earth.

earth, 1 Chr 28:2, cf. Psa 99:5, 132:7, Lam 2:1. A similar image to Ezek 43:7a is found in Isa 60:13:

> ¹³*The glory of Lebanon shall come to you,*
> *the cypress, the plane, and the pine,*
> **to beautify the place of my sanctuary,**
> **and I will make the place of my feet glorious.**

In Ezekiel 43:7a and Isa 60:13, however, we are seeing the throne of God *and* His "footstool" to be *one place, on the earth*.[12] That this is "Zion," even though Ezekiel declines to call it that, is clear from parallels elsewhere in the Prophets, such as Jer 3:12-18:

> ¹²*Go, and proclaim these words toward the north, and say,*
>> *"'Return, faithless Israel,*
>> *declares the L*ORD*.*
> *I will not look on you in anger,*
>> *for I am merciful,*
> *declares the L*ORD*;*
>> *I will not be angry forever.*
> ¹³*Only acknowledge your guilt,*
>> *that you rebelled against the L*ORD *your God*
> *and scattered your favors among foreigners*
>> *under every green tree,*
> *and that you have not obeyed my voice,*
>> *declares the L*ORD*.*
> ¹⁴*Return, O faithless children,*
>> *declares the L*ORD*;*
> *for I am your master;*

---

[12] As noted in footnote 10, the decision to "interpret" the location of the eschatological temple or sanctuary as on *earth* (but the "new earth," of 2 Pet 3:13 and Rev 21:1 is not arbitrary, but is driven by scriptural exegesis. For a fuller discussion, see footnote 74.

> *I will take you, one from a city and two from a family, and **I will bring you to Zion**.*
> ¹⁵*"'And I will give you shepherds after my own heart, who will feed you with knowledge and understanding. ¹⁶And when you have multiplied and been fruitful in the land, **in those days**, declares the LORD, **they shall no more say, "The ark of the covenant of the LORD."** It shall not come to mind or be remembered or missed; it shall not be made again. ¹⁷**At that time Jerusalem shall be called the throne of the LORD, and all nations shall gather to it, to the presence of the LORD in Jerusalem**, and they shall no more stubbornly follow their own evil heart. ¹⁸In those days **the house of Judah shall join the house of Israel**, and together they shall come from the land of the north to the land that I gave your fathers for a heritage.*

No longer will Yahweh's presence *on earth* be limited to the Ark of the Covenant (e.g., the inner sanctum of the Temple), but will then be associated with the entire city of Jerusalem. It is Zion, but a new Zion, a new Jerusalem, that will host "the throne of God" *on earth* in the coming age ("in those days" and "at that time").

It is equally important to an understanding of Old Testament prophecy to understand the significance of the theme of reunification of Judah and Israel that we see in Jer 3:18. In Ezek 37:15-28 we have a similar promise of a unification of Israel and Judah. In Ezek 37:15-19 the LORD tells Ezekiel to take two sticks and write "For Judah, and the people of Israel associated with him" on one of the sticks, and "For Joseph (the stick of Ephraim) and all of the house of Israel associated with him" on the other, and then to join them together as one stick in his hand. The

Lord GOD then says that He will join the two sticks together and make them one stick, that they may be one in His hand.

Then in vv. 20-23 we read:

> [20] When the sticks on which you write are in your hand before their eyes, [21] then say to them, Thus says the Lord GOD: Behold, I will take the people of Israel from the nations among which they have gone, and will gather them from all around, and bring them to their own land. [22] And **I will make them one nation in the land, on the mountains of Israel.** And one king shall be king over them all, **and they shall be no longer two nations, and no longer divided into two kingdoms.** [23] They shall not defile themselves anymore with their idols and their detestable things, or with any of their transgressions. But I will save them from all the backslidings in which they have sinned, and will cleanse them; **and they shall be my people, and I will be their God.**

What is important to understand about this reunification of Judah and Israel is that it never took place during the time of the Old Testament. These are not prophesies and promises related to the *physical* nation of Israel, but to the *spiritual* nation of Israel, those who are descendants of Abraham *by faith* and not by *blood*, Rom 9:6-8, Gal 3:29, 4:28. In Rom 9:25-26 Paul cites two passages from the book of Hosea (1:10 and 2:23) and applies them to the salvation of Gentiles. In Hosea, the passages appear to refer to the eventual restoration of Israel (as in the northern Kingdom, often referred to as Ephraim in Hosea). In applying these prophecies to the salvation of the Gentiles, Paul indicates that the Old Testament promises of a reunion of Israel and Judah as a united kingdom were not literal, but figurative, representing the union of Jew and Gentile in Christ as a new, *spiritual* Israel, Gal 6:16, cf. Rom 2:29, Phil 3:3. Peter, too, understood Hos 2:23 to be prophetic of the salvation of Gentiles, 1 Pet 2:10. So, whenever we see Old Testament prophecy speak of a re-unification of Judah and Israel, this refers not to the literal nations or kingdoms of ethnic Jews, but to the union of Jew and Gentile in Christ to create a new humanity.

To bring this promise of a reunified Israel back around to the promise of God to be in the midst of his people are the final verses of Ezek 37, vv. 24-28:

> [24] *"**My servant David** shall be king over them, and they shall all have one shepherd. They shall walk in my rules and be careful to obey my statutes. [25]They shall dwell in the land that I gave to my servant Jacob, where your fathers lived. They and their children and their children's children shall dwell there forever, and **David my servant shall be their prince forever**.*
> [26]*I will make **a covenant of peace** with them. It shall be an **everlasting covenant** with them. And I will set them in their land and multiply them, and will **set my sanctuary in their midst forevermore**. [27]My dwelling place shall be with them, and **I will be their God, and they shall be my people**. [28]Then the nations will know that I am the* LORD *who sanctifies Israel, **when my sanctuary is in their midst forevermore**."*

The messianic focus of Ezek 37:15-28 – that it refers to the new humanity created in Christ, and not to ethnic Israel – is unmistakable. And like the texts we considered at the beginning of this chapter, here too the focus is upon Yahweh dwelling *in the midst* of His creation, and of

His people.

The Hebrew word for "in the midst" is *tāvek*.[13] It is a common word, but takes on theological significance in contexts where it is associated with God being with, or dwelling with, His people. This significance is sometimes obscured by the fact that *tāvek* is often translated "among," such that the English reader is left unaware that different passages are using the same Hebrew word. A case in point, from two texts that independently attest to the theological significance of *tāvek* in connection with God dwelling with His people, is Exod 25:8 and Lev 26:11-12:

> [8]*And let them make me a sanctuary, that I may dwell **in their midst** [tāvek].*

> [11]*I will make my dwelling **among** [tāvek] you, and my soul shall not abhor you.* [12]*And I will walk **among** [tāvek] you and will be your God, and you shall be my people.*

Grammatically, the only difference between the use of *tāvek* in Exod 25:8 and Lev 26:11-12 is that the first is third person plural, while the second is second person plural. It would be perfectly acceptable to translate the Leviticus passage "I will make my dwelling *in your midst*...and I will walk *in your midst*."

The theological significance of this motif is even earlier than Exodus and Leviticus; we find it describing God's presence in Eden in Gen 3:8:

> [8]*And they heard the sound of the* LORD *God **walking** in the garden in the cool of the day, and the man and his wife hid themselves from the presence of the*

---

[13] Strong's #H1980.

LORD *God among the trees of the garden.*

The presence of Yahweh *in the garden* has frequently been understood to signify that Eden was a type of "temple," a place on earth where God "tabernacles" with His creation. We will say a bit more about this later (pp. 32-33).

For now, not to be overlooked is the reference to God "walking," both in Lev 26:12 and Gen 3:8, where the word "walk" is used in a grammatical form that signifies sovereignty or dominion.[14] The juxtaposition of Yahweh "walking in the midst" of His people occurs also in Deut 23:14:

> [14]*Because the* LORD *your God* **walks** [hālak] **in the midst** [tāvek] *of your camp, to deliver you and to give up your enemies before you, therefore your camp must be holy, so that he may not see anything indecent among you and turn away from you.*

What is most significant about all of this is that it does not just describe the LORD's desire to walk and be among or in the midst of His people, but that this close communion between God and man is set, or takes place, *on the earth.* Gen 3:8, and especially Lev 26:11-12, make direct intertextual links forward to Ezek 37:26-28, and from there forward to Rev 21:3:

> [3]*And I heard a loud voice from the throne saying, "Behold,* **the dwelling place of God is with man.** *He will dwell with them, and* **they will be his people,** *and* **God himself will be with them as their God.**

---

[14] The Hebrew *hālak*, Strong's #H1980, in the Hithpael stem "views walking or stepping as tantamount to the exercise of sovereignty," NIDOTTE, 1: 1034, 6 (specifically noting Gen 3:8).

That Rev 21:3 represents the fulfillment and consummation of the Old Testament texts about God being among or dwelling in the midst of His people is *beyond reasonable doubt*.

Note well the following parallels:

> Lev 26:11 **I will make my dwelling** [*miškān*] **among** [*tāvek*] **you**
> Rev 21:3 **Behold the dwelling place** [*skēnē*] **of God is among** [*meta*] **men**[15]
> Ezek 37:27 **My dwelling place** [*miškān*] **shall be with them**, *and I will be their God, and they shall be my people.*
> Rev 21:3 **He will dwell** [*skēnoō*] **with them, *and they will be his people*, and God** himself **will be with them as their God.**

The Hebrew word translated "dwelling," *miškān*, and the Greek word translated "dwelling place," *skēnē*, are the Hebrew and Greek words typically translated as "tabernacle." The Greek translated "will dwell," *skēnoō*, could be translated "will tabernacle with them." What we have in Rev 21:1-3, then, is the consummation and fulfillment of Old Testament prophecy regarding Zion and Jerusalem as the place *on earth* where God will choose to dwell *in the midst* of His creation and His people. Not the place associated literally with Zion and Jerusalem during the Old Testament, but a place where all things are being made *new*, Rev 21:5, i.e., a *new Zion* and a

---

[15] I have substituted the NASB (1995) reading "among men" for the ESV's "with man." Why the ESV chose to translate *anthrōpōn* (men) as singular is baffling. Other versions translating *meta* as "among" include the NET Bible, NIV, and NRSV.

new Jerusalem associated with a new cosmos, *new heavens and a new earth*, Rev 21:1, cf. 2 Pet 3:13, Isa 65:17, 66:22. The direction of "movement" and the location of "place" are very clear in Rev 21:2-3. God is *coming* to a *place* that is not in Heaven (e.g., it is "out of Heaven"), and He is dwelling with His people, *where they dwell*; they have not gone to Heaven, to dwell where He dwells. We will have more to say about this "coming of God" in chapter 5.

3 THE MOUNTAIN OF GOD

That Jerusalem and Zion were known as "the mountain of God" in the Old Testament, and are depicted as the eternal dwelling place of the redeemed in Revelation 21-22, tells us something about the nature of the *place* where the redeemed will dwell for eternity: *on earth* (the *new earth*), and not *in Heaven*.[16] Mountains are geomorphological features of earth, not Heaven. More than that, they often have theological significance as places that *connect* Heaven and earth, places where the divine meets the mundane.

The association of deity with mountains was common in ancient near east religions. Similarities in this respect between the Baal religion of the Canaanites and the Zion traditions of the Hebrew Bible are often taken to imply

---

[16] Similar depictions of Jerusalem and Zion include "His/my/the holy mountain," Psa 48:1, 99:9, Isa 11:9, 27:3, 65:11, 25, 66:20, Ezek 20:40, Joel 2:1, 3:17, Zech 8:3, and "the mountain of the LORD/the house of the LORD/of hosts," Isa 2:2-3, 30:29, Mic 4:1-2, Zech 8:3.

that the former influenced the latter. But this association of deity with mountains is so widespread, and is found in religions with little or no contact with Old Testament traditions, that it is far more likely that this association goes back to a common, earlier, *reality*.

Within the Old Testament itself, we see this association found "in the beginning," i.e., in *Eden*. In Ezekiel 28 we find a prophecy of judgment and lament against the king of Tyre. In vv. 11-16 we find the king of Tyre being compared to someone who was present in the beginning, in the garden of Eden:

> ^{11}*Moreover, the word of the L*ORD *came to me:*
> ^{12}*"Son of man, raise a lamentation over the king of Tyre, and say to him, Thus says the Lord G*OD*:*
>> *"You were the signet of perfection,*
>>> *full of wisdom and perfect in beauty.*
>> ^{13}*You were **in Eden, the garden of God**;*
>>> *every precious stone was your covering,*
>> *sardius, topaz, and diamond,*
>>> *beryl, onyx, and jasper,*
>> *sapphire, emerald, and carbuncle;*
>>> *and crafted in gold were your settings*
>> *and your engravings.*
>> *On the day that you were created*
>> *they were prepared.*
>> ^{14}*You were an anointed guardian cherub.*
>>> *I placed you; you were **on the holy mountain of** *
>> ***God**; in the midst of the stones of fire you walked.*
>> ^{15}*You were blameless in your ways*
>>> *from the day you were created,*
>> *till unrighteousness was found in you.*
>> ^{16}*In the abundance of your trade*
>>> *you were filled with violence in your midst,*

> *and you sinned; so I cast you as a profane thing*
> *from **the mountain of God**,*
> *and I destroyed you, O guardian cherub,*
> *from the midst of the stones of fire.*

The "person" in the garden to whom the king of Tyre is being compared is uncertain, though the identity does not impact the point we will be making. As to the possibilities, there are only two: either Adam, or Satan. Plausible arguments can be advanced for either. If I were forced to choose, I would choose Adam as the one who is being described here.

The reason for calling attention to this text is to show that *Eden* was the *original* "mountain of God." While not called "the mountain of God" in Genesis 2 and 3, the location depicted in Gen 2:11-14 places Eden at the *headwaters* of the four rivers that flowed *out* of it.[17] The biblical Eden was most certainly located in a geologically or geomorphologically *elevated* region, i.e., on or in "the mountains." Thus, the widespread association of mountains with deity can be explained simply as the result of the Bible's own creation story. The original "mountain of God" was the original home of humanity, the garden of Eden, a place where God *and* humanity once lived together in harmony and peace. Thus, we have now pushed Zion's story back to the very beginning of creation.

---

[17] This seems to rule out *completely* any theory of the historical location of Eden near the *confluence* of the Tigris and Euphrates River in what is now southern Iraq. While geomorphological and geological changes wrought by the Genesis flood make certainty regarding the antediluvian location of Eden impossible, a location proximate with the headwaters of those two rivers closer to the mountainous eastern Anatolia (modern Turkey) is far more likely.

Scholars of religion sometimes refer to the archetypal association between mountains and deity as "the cosmic mountain." Inherent in the term is the idea that mountains are where "heaven" and "earth" meet. We see this in the story of Babel in Genesis 11 (vv. 1-9). After the flood, people migrated to the *plain* (flatland) in the land of Shinar. With no mountains rising toward the heavens, the people decided to build a tower that would reach to the heavens. When "the LORD came down to see the tower and the city, which the children of man had built," v. 5, He saw a reprise of the same human hubris that led to the conditions resulting in the destruction of the world in the Genesis flood, and He confused the languages of men such as to cause a linguistic and ethnic dispersion of humanity.[18] Where "heaven" and "earth" meet is the prerogative of God, not man!

The "cosmic mountain" idea is closely related to the concept of an "axis mundi," Latin for the "axis of the world," an axis connecting the poles of the earth along a line that connects heaven and earth. This is *not* the literal axis around which the *geophysical* earth rotates, but a spiritual axis connecting heaven and earth. The "cosmic mountain" resides along this "axis mundi" at "the *navel* of the earth." This pertains to our topic because Jews of the Old Testament period believed that Jerusalem/Zion (as the center of the land of Israel) was the center of the world, the navel of the earth. The basis for this belief

---

[18] Chronologically, Gen 11:1-9 follows directly after Genesis 9, and before the "Table of Nations" of Genesis 10. It is an "afterword" that explains the widespread geographical dispersion of the descendants of Noah's three sons and their 70 grandsons.

came from Ezek 5:5 and 38:12:

Ezek 5:5

⁵*"Thus says the Lord GOD: This is **Jerusalem. I have set her in the center of the nations**, with countries all around her.*

Ezek 38:12

¹²*to seize spoil and carry off plunder, to turn your hand against the waste places that are now inhabited, and the people who were gathered from the nations, who have acquired livestock and goods, **who dwell at the center of the earth**.*[19]

The Hebrew word translated "center" [of the earth] in Ezek 38:12 is *ṭabûr*, which is sometimes translated "navel."[20] When the Hebrew Old Testament was translated into the Greek (the Septuagint, or LXX), *ṭabûr* was translated *omphalos*, the Greek word for "navel" associated with a religious stone artifact at Delphi and believed by the Greeks to be the center of the earth. That the translators of the LXX chose the Greek word *omphalos* to translate *ṭabûr* may be associated with the belief that the Temple Mount and the Foundation Stone (now covered

---

[19] The context of Ezekiel 38 and 39 is that of a last, eschatological, end-time battle with the nations aligned against God's people. The exiles have returned to Zion, and attempt is made to defeat God and his people, those "who dwell at the center ["navel"] of the earth," i.e., Zion. In chapter 6 we associate this with the "last days" of the New Testament.

[20] The Briggs-Driver-Brown lexicon renders the relevant phrase in Ezek 38:12 as "dwelling upon the navel of the earth," adding, "i.e., upon the mountainous country of Israel, central and prominent in the earth." BDB, 371, Strong's #H2872.

by the Dome of the Rock) is located where land first appeared, Gen 1:9, and was the original location of the garden of Eden.

In the apocryphal Book of Jubilees, the eighth chapter is a retelling of the Genesis 10 account of how the earth was divided among the sons of Noah. Verse 19 reads:

> And he [Noah] *knew that the Garden of Eden is the holy of holies, and the dwelling of the Lord, and Mount Sinai the centre of the desert, and Mount Zion – the centre of the navel of the earth: these three were created as holy places facing each other.*[21]

Ancient maps often depicted Zion or Jerusalem at the center of the earth. The Madaba Map, a floor mosaic in a Byzantine church in Madaba, Jordan, built in the 6th century, depicts Jerusalem as the center of the earth, but specifically with the Holy Church of the Sepulcher, the traditional site of Golgotha, rather than the Temple Mount.

Despite the obvious speculative nature of much of this, especially as it relates to the location of the garden of Eden, the depiction of Eden as the "mountain of God" in Ezekiel 28 is undeniable. And what is significant about this is that the place where God will dwell, eternally, in the midst of His people, i.e., Zion, is called the mountain of God also. And again, mountains are earthly features, not heavenly ones (at least as the word "heavenly" is often

---

[21] The writer of the Book of Jubilees was not among those colocating Eden with Jerusalem. In the geography of Jubilees 8, the garden of Eden is at the easternmost edge of the world, not the center of it, like Zion. The 14th century Herford Mappa Mundi also depicted Jerusalem as the center of the world, and Eden at the easternmost edge of the world, inaccessible to the rest of the world.

used in this context).²² Thus the following passages, affirming an eternal dwelling place for God in Zion, the mountain of God, speak to an eternal dwelling place for the LORD *on earth* (but a "new earth," Isa 65:17, 66:22, 2 Pet 3:13, Rev 21:1), not in Heaven:

Psa 68:16
¹⁶*Why do you look with hatred, O many-peaked mountain, at **the mount that God desired for his abode, yes, where the LORD will dwell forever***?

Psa 125:1-2
¹*Those who trust in the LORD are like **Mount Zion**,*
   which cannot be moved, but abides forever.
²*As the mountains surround Jerusalem,*
   so the LORD surrounds his people,
from this time forth and forevermore.

Psa 132:13-17
¹³*For **the LORD has chosen Zion;***
   he has desired it for his dwelling place:
¹⁴*"**This is my resting place forever;***

---

²² Among those who believe that the eternal abode of the righteous is to dwell with God *in Heaven*, some say that "heavenly" always refers to place or location, not to origin, citing verses such as 2 Tim 4:18, and Heb 6:4, 11:16, 12:22-23. However, the lexicons agree that as an adjective the Greek word for "heavenly" (*ouranios*, Strong's #G3770) is not limited to meaning "in Heaven" but can refer to that which pertains to, originates in, or is *from* Heaven:

   related to or located in heaven – heavenly, in heaven, pertaining to Heaven, LN, 2:4, 1.12;

   belonging to heaven, coming from or living in heaven, heavenly, BDAG, 737;

   dwelling in heaven, ... b. coming from heaven, Thayer, 464.

To insist, for example, that the "heavenly" Jerusalem of Heb 12:22 can *only* refer to a Jerusalem "in" Heaven would directly contradict Rev 3:12, 21:2, 10.

> **here I will dwell, for I have desired it.**
> ¹⁵*I will abundantly bless her provisions;*
>   *I will satisfy her poor with bread.*
> ¹⁶ *Her priests I will clothe with salvation,*
> *and her saints will shout for joy.*[23]
> ¹⁷*There I will make a horn to sprout for David;*
>   *I have prepared a lamp for my anointed.*[24]

Ezek 43:7, 9

> ⁷*and he said to me, "Son of man, this is the place of my throne and the place of the soles of my feet, where **I will dwell in the midst of the people of Israel forever**. And the house of Israel shall no more defile my holy name, neither they, nor their kings, by their whoring and by the dead bodies of their kings at their high places...* ⁹*Now let them put away their whoring and the dead bodies of their kings far from me, and **I will dwell in their midst forever**.*

Lastly, the colocation of Eden and the "mountain of God" as a place where God originally dwelt in the midst of His creation indicates that it was the original *sanctuary* or temple of God on earth. More or less by definition, a sanctuary or temple is a place where *deity dwells*. So Heaven is sometimes depicted as a temple or sanctuary, Psa 11:4, 102:19 (KJV, ASV, NIV, NET Bible), cf. Heb 9:24, Rev 11:19. And the most holy place or inner sanctum of the Tabernacle and Temple were places where deity dwelt. It has often been noted that the tripartite design of the Tabernacle was a *microcosm* of the *cosmos* itself, with the outer court representing earth, the holy place

---

[23] In Christ all the redeemed ("saints") represent a kingdom of priests, Rev 1:6, cf. Rev 5:10, 20:6, 1 Pet 2:9.

[24] This is an obvious messianic promise, fulfilled in Christ.

representing the celestial realm, and the most holy place representing Heaven.[25] But Heaven *itself* is not "in the midst" of creation. It is "high above" the nations of the earth, Psa 113:4, cf. Psa 92:8, 93:4, 113:5, and the "highest" of the heavens, Deut 10:14, Neh 9:6. In Biblical cosmology, the cosmos is represented vertically, with Heaven *above* the rest of creation (not "in the midst" of it), the *starry* heavens above the earth, the earth *in the center* of the Biblical cosmos, and the realm of the dead *below* the earth.[26] All of the language about God dwelling *in the midst* of His people is, in the end, about dwelling with them *on earth*, not in Heaven. In the next chapter we take a closer look at the relationship between what is being said here about the LORD, in the age to come, dwelling in the midst of His people on (a new) *earth*.

---

[25] The Jewish writers Josephus and Philo drew comparisons between the Tabernacle and the cosmos along similar lines. Among later writers the comparison was more explicit.

[26] This depiction is *phenomenological*, meaning that it depicts things as they "appear" to be, not necessarily as they "are." When someone says that the sun rises in the morning, and sets in the evening, that is a "phenomenological" description. No one mistakes it (since the time of Galileo) as a "scientific" description. Scripture describes Hades as "under" or "beneath" the earth because we "bury" people in the earth; but Hades is a *spiritual* realm, and is not "really" under the earth. The Biblical description of the cosmos is phenomenological and not intended to be "scientific."

ZION'S STORY

4 TO DWELL FOREVER IN ZION

At the end of the previous chapter, we took a brief look at four texts that speak of Yahweh dwelling in Zion forever: Psa 68:16, 125:1-2, 132:13-17, Ezek 43:7, 9. The last is clearly eschatological, an end-time vision of a final epoch (age) in which the LORD will dwell in the midst of His people forever. The historical settings of the three passages from Psalms are more complex. There is every reason to believe that many of the Psalms were adapted (what scholars sometimes call "redacted") over time to meet the liturgical need of Israel at different points in time. This is sometimes relevant to a proper understanding of their eschatological significance.

Psalm 68, for instance, is attributed to David, and there is little (if anything) in the first 27 or 28 verses of the Psalm that could not fit a setting during the time of David. But in verses 29 and 31 we read:

[29]*Because of **your temple at Jerusalem***

> *kings shall bear gifts to you.*
> ³¹*Nobles **shall come from Egypt;***
> ***Cush shall hasten to stretch out her hands to God.***

The mention of the Temple in Jerusalem in v. 29 is clearly out of place for a setting during the time of David, and v. 31 reads like something we might find in the prophetic books of the Old Testament, such as:

Isa 45:14
> ¹⁴*Thus says the LORD:*
> ***"The wealth of Egypt and the merchandise of Cush,***
> *and the Sabeans, men of stature,*
>   *shall come over to you and be yours;*
> *they shall follow you;*
>   *they shall come over in chains and bow down to you.*
> *They will plead with you, saying:*
>   *'Surely God is in you, and there is no other,*
> *no god besides him.'"*

Zeph 3:9-10, 14-17, 20
> ⁹*"For at that time I will change the speech of the peoples*
>   *to a pure speech,*
>   *that all of them may call upon the name of the LORD*
>   *and serve him with one accord.*
> ¹⁰ ***From beyond the rivers of Cush***
>   *my worshipers, the daughter of my dispersed ones,*
>   *shall bring my offering.*
> ¹⁴*Sing aloud, **O Daughter Zion**;*²⁷
>   *shout, O Israel!*
> *Rejoice and exult with all your heart,*
>   *O Daughter Jerusalem!*¹⁶
> ¹⁵*The LORD has taken away the judgments against you;*

---

²⁷ The ESV's "daughter of" has been changed to "Daughter" as in the NET Bible. For an explanation, see footnotes 7 and 8.

> *he has cleared away your enemies.*
> *The King of Israel, the* LORD, **is in your midst;**
> *you shall never again fear evil.*
> ¹⁶*On that day it shall be said to Jerusalem:*
> *"Fear not,* **O Zion;**
> *let not your hands grow weak.*
> ¹⁷*The* LORD *your God* **is in your midst,**
> *a mighty one who will save;*
> *he will rejoice over you with gladness;*
> *he will quiet you by his love;*
> *he will exult over you with loud singing.*
> ²⁰*At that* **time I will bring you in,**
> **at the time when I gather you together;**
> *for I will make you renowned and praised*
> *among all the peoples of the earth,*
> *when I* **restore your fortunes**
> *before your eyes," says the* LORD.

Isa 45:14 and Zeph 3:9-10 allude to the end-time conversion of the Nations (i.e., Gentiles), which we address more directly in the next chapter. Zeph 3:14-17, 20 puts this in the context of the time when Yahweh has returned to Zion, to once again being *in the midst* of His people (after having departed the Temple in 587 BC). What was originally a Psalm set during the time of David has been adapted for a later liturgical (worship) setting reflecting an eschatological hope that will come to pass in the time of the Messiah.[28] And thus, the setting is one that is suitable for *us* to study, meditate, and reflect upon regarding

---

[28] There is nothing in the preceding sentence that is incompatible with a high view of the inspiration of scripture. As we have it, Psalm 68 comes to us in its *canonical form*, i.e., the form by which it was received into the Old Testament canon by the community of faith

our own eschatological hope.

Psalms 125 and 132 are two of the "Songs of Ascents" which reflect exilic or post-exilic settings, and are thus contemporary with the eschatological and messianic hope found in the Prophets, such as in the last of the four passages we looked at the end of the previous chapter from the prophet Ezekiel, Ezek 43:7, 9.

In reflecting on the eschatological and messianic hope reflected in the Psalms and the Prophets with respect to Zion's story, we should take heart of what Peter said to the crowd that formed in Solomon's Portico after he healed the lame man in Acts 3:19-21:

> [19]*Repent therefore, and turn back, that your sins may be blotted out,* [20]*that times of refreshing may come from the presence of the Lord, and that he may* **send the Christ** *appointed for you, Jesus,* [21]*whom heaven must receive* **until the time for restoring all the things about which God spoke by the mouth of his holy prophets long ago.**

Peter is saying that our own eschatological hope (what will happen when Christ returns) is the same hope "for

---

that canonized the Old Testament as it has come down to us today. If we consider the Old Testament as we have it as the word of God, we must believe that the Holy Spirit was just as involved in any redaction and final selection into the canon as He was in inspiring David to write it as it existed in David's time. According to Jewish tradition Ezra and the "Great Assembly" (what later became the Sanhedrin) gave the Psalms their canonical form. That may or may not be so. All that matters is that we understand that in their canonical form, some Psalms which may have had an original composition and purpose relating to an earlier time in Israel's history, have been adapted to reflect an eschatological and messianic focus and hope.

restoring all the things" that God "spoke by the mouth of his holy prophets" in the Old Testament. This does not just *warrant* our close attention to the eschatological hope revealed in the Old Testament, it well-nigh *demands* it.

We cannot know how much David himself understood about the resurrection, but he seems to have had a nascent understanding of an eschatological future for God's people.[29] In Psalm 37, vv. 1-11, 18-20, 22, 27-29, 34, we find David saying:

> *^{1}Fret not yourself because of evildoers;*
> *be not envious of wrongdoers!*
> *^{2}For* **they shall soon fade like the grass**
> *and wither like the green herb.*
> *^{3}Trust in the* LORD*, and do good;*
> **dwell in the land** *and befriend faithfulness.*
> *^{4}Delight yourself in the* LORD*,*
> *and he will give you the desires of your heart.*
> *^{5}Commit your way to the* LORD*;*
> *trust in him, and* **he will act.**
> *^{6}He* **will bring forth your righteousness** *as the light,*
> **and your justice** *as the noonday.*
> *^{7}Be still before the* LORD *and* **wait patiently for him;**
> *fret not yourself over the one who prospers in his way,*
> *over the man who carries out evil devices!*

---

[29] I am not referring here to things he might have written under the power of inspiration, like Psa 16:10 or 110:1, which took on new meaning or understanding after the death and resurrection of Jesus. As Peter tells us in 1 Pet 1:10-12, Old Testament prophets (a category that would include David) did not always understand the full import of what was being revealed through their writings and utterances. In the text above I am thinking more in terms of what David *did* himself understand or believe about things to come.

Zion's Story

⁸Refrain from anger, and forsake wrath!
  Fret not yourself; it tends only to evil.
⁹For the **evildoers shall be cut off,**
  but those who **wait for the LORD** shall **inherit the land.**
¹⁰**In just a little while, the wicked will be no more;**
  though you look carefully at his place, he
  will not be there.
¹¹**But the meek shall inherit the land**
  and delight themselves in abundant peace.
¹⁸The LORD knows the days of the blameless,
  and **their inheritance**[30] **will remain forever;**
¹⁹they are not put to shame in evil times;
  in the days of famine they have abundance.
²⁰But **the wicked will perish;** the enemies of the LORD
  are like the glory of the pastures;
  they vanish—like smoke they vanish away.
²²for those blessed by the LORD shall **inherit the land,**
  but **those cursed by him shall be cut off.**
²⁷Turn away from evil and do good;
  so shall you **dwell forever.**
²⁸For the LORD loves **justice;**
  he **will not forsake** his saints.
 They are **preserved forever,**
  but the children of the **wicked shall be cut off.**
²⁹The righteous shall **inherit the land**
  and **dwell upon it forever.**
³⁴**Wait for the LORD** and keep his way,
  and he will exalt you to **inherit the land;**
  you will look on when **the wicked are cut off.**

---

[30] I have substituted "inheritance" here (per KJV, ASV, NASB, NIV, NET Bible, and many others) for the ESV's "heritage" to make the connection to "inherit" found in vv. 9, 11, 22, 29 and 34 more apparent.

An eschatological focus for this Psalm is apparent for several reasons.

First, there is the focus upon *waiting, a little while,* for something (vv. 7, 9, 10, 34). And what the righteous are waiting for is a (future[31]) time when: 1) the LORD *will act* to *bring forth righteousness* and *justice* (vv. 5, 6, 28); 2) evildoers, wrongdoers, and the wicked will *fade like grass, be cut off, be no more, not be there, perish, vanish away like smoke* (vv. 2, 9, 10, 20, 22, 28, 34); 3) and the righteous will be *preserved, not be forsaken* and will receive an *inheritance* (vv. 9, 11, 18, 22, 29, 34; that 4) will last *forever* (vv. 18, 27-29). Themes found in the major and minor Prophets about an eschatological future for God's people are thus pervasive in this Psalm.

Now, what is this promised *inheritance* of Psalm 37? It is "the land" (vv. 3, 9, 11, 22, 29, 34). The quotes are required because the Hebrew word for "land," *'ereṣ*, is also often translated "earth," and this may prove significant later. Here, in this context, "the land" would seem appropriate as alluding to "the land" that was considered the promised inheritance to the offspring of the Patriarchs (Abraham, Isaac, and Jacob), Gen 12:6-9, 13:14-17, 15:18-19, 17:8 (Abraham), 26:3-5 (Isaac), 28:4, 13-15 (Jacob). But the return from Babylonian captivity failed to live up to the expectations created by Israel's prophetic writings. When Daniel prayed that Jerusalem's "desolations" might come to an end with the return to the land after 70 years of captivity foretold by Jeremiah, Dan 9:2-3, he was told in a vision by Gabriel that "desolations are decreed" for

---

[31] In 19 verses, the future tense "will" and "shall" occur 19 times.

"Seventy weeks" (of years, i.e., 7x70=490). Even Ezra recognized that the rebuilding of the walls of the city and the Temple after the return from Babylonian captivity were only a "brief moment" granting "a little reviving," but left them slaves under foreign rule by kings set over them because of their sins, Ezra 9:8-9, Neh 9:36-37. Haggai records how the rebuilt temple could not compare to the glory of the former temple, and that there would be a *yet future temple* in which the "latter glory of this house shall be greater than the former," Hag 2:6-9. In Luke 2, the stories of Simeon (vv. 25-32) and Anna (vv. 36-38) stand as witnesses to how a faithful remnant in Israel had come to understand that the great and wonderful promises in the later Prophets were pointing to a future that would be far more radical than just a *status quo* return to the land occupied by Israel during the time of the United Kingdom under David and Solomon.

Careful reading of the eschatological hopes in the Psalms and the later Prophets point to a time when *all the earth* would be blessed, not just the land occupied during the United Kingdom. If Psalm 1 stands as a header or introduction to the Psalms as *wisdom* literature, Psalm 2 announces a program of *eschatological* promise under one who would be "the LORD's Anointed," i.e., "Messiah," who would reign as King from "Zion, [Yahweh's] holy hill, vv. 2, 6-8:

> ²*The kings of the earth set themselves,*
>   *and the rulers take counsel together,*
>   *against the LORD and against his Anointed...*
> ⁶*"As for me, I have set my* **King**

> *on Zion, my holy hill."*
> *⁷I will tell of the decree:*
> *The LORD said to me, "You are my Son;*
> *today I have begotten you.*
> *⁸Ask of me, and **I will make the nations your inheritance**,*³²
> *and **the ends of the earth your possession**.*

Note well that the *inheritance* of the King who reigns from Zion will not simply be the land promised to Israel after the conquest of Canaan, but will include *all the nations* and that his reign will extend to *the ends of the earth*.

A very similar promise appears in Zech 9:9-10:

> *⁹Rejoice greatly, O Daughter Zion!*
> *Shout aloud, O Daughter Jerusalem!*³³
> *Behold, your **king** is coming to you;*
> *righteous and having salvation is he,*
> *humble and mounted on a donkey,*
> *on a colt, the foal of a donkey.*
> *¹⁰I will cut off the chariot from Ephraim*
> *and the war horse from Jerusalem;*
> *and the battle bow shall be cut off,*
> *and he shall **speak peace to the nations**;*
> ***his rule** shall be from sea to sea,*
> *and from the River **to the ends of the earth**.*

Verse 9 will be familiar from its quotation in the New Testament, Matt 21:15, John 12:15. Verse 10 tells us that Zion's King will "speak peace to the nations" and that his rule will encompass *the whole earth*.

---

³² As in Psa 37:18 (see footnote 30) I have substituted "inheritance" for the ESV's "heritage."

³³ I have changed the ESV's "daughter of Zion/Jerusalem" to "Daughter Zion/Jerusalem." Cf. NIV, NRSV, and others, and footnotes 7 and 8.

Zion's Story

This inclusion of the nations in the kingdom of the King of Zion is an important part of "the return to Zion," a theme explored the next chapter. Here we are simply showing that the promised inheritance of the Lord's Anointed, King of Zion, would not be limited to the land of Canaan, but would encompass the whole earth. The King of Zion, the Lord's Anointed, shares in the reign of the Lord over all the earth:

Psa 47:1-2, 7
> ¹*Clap your hands, all peoples!*
>   *Shout to God with loud songs of joy!*
> ²*For the Lord, the Most High, is to be feared,*
>   *a great **king over all the earth**.*
> ⁷*For God is **the King of all the earth**;*
>   *sing praises with a psalm!*

Psa 99:2
> ²*The Lord is great **in Zion**;*
>   *he is **exalted over all the peoples**.*

Psa 96:7-13
> ⁷*Ascribe to the Lord, O **families of the peoples**,*
>   *ascribe to the Lord glory and strength!*
> ⁸*Ascribe to the Lord the glory due his name;*
>   *bring an offering, and come into his courts!*
> ⁹*Worship the Lord in the splendor of holiness;*
>   *tremble before him, **all the earth**!*
> ¹⁰*Say **among the nations**, "**The Lord reigns**!*
>   *Yes, **the world is established; it shall never be moved**;*
>   *he will **judge the peoples** with equity."*
> ¹¹***Let the heavens be glad, and let the earth rejoice**;*
>   *let the sea roar, and all that fills it;*
> ¹²*let the field exult, and everything in it!*
>   *Then shall all the trees of the forest sing for joy*

> ¹³*before the LORD, **for he comes,***
> ***for he comes to judge the earth.***
> ***He will judge the world in righteousness,***
> ***and the peoples in his faithfulness.***

Zech 14:9
> ⁹*And the LORD will be **king over all the earth**. On that day the LORD will be one and his name one.*

Psa 96:7-13 is an important text for our study. Its eschatological focus is indicated by the language about "coming" (v. 13) and "judgment" (vv. 10, 13). And the coming judgment will be upon the "world/earth" and "the peoples." The Hebrew word translated "world," *tēḇēl*, is most often used, especially in poetry, as a synonym for "earth" (*'ereṣ*).³⁴ That the "earth" or "world" is being judged does not suggest anything sinister with respect to the future of the world or earth. To the contrary, "the world is established, it shall *never* be moved" (v. 10) and this coming of Yahweh in judgment is a time of *rejoicing* for God's material creation (vv. 11-12).³⁵ The picture here is radically different than the modern eschatological view of the earth and all of creation (except humanity) being *annihilated* in the Day of Judgment. But truth be told, the concept of an annihilation of creation would have been unthinkable to any Jew of the Second Temple or New Testament times with a knowledge of what the

---

³⁴ Strong's #H8398. Cf. NIDOTTE, 4:273:
> It is used frequently in contexts that associate it with Yahweh's creative act and that, as a result, express the stability or durability of the earth (1 Sam 2:8; Ps 89:11[12]; 93:1, 96:10).

³⁵ In the New Testament, a similar theme regarding creation is found in Rom 8:18-25.

Hebrew scriptures taught about the *eternity of creation*.[36]

We began this chapter recalling a quartet of passages under discussion at the end of the previous chapter: Psa 68:16, 125:1-2, 132:13-17, Ezek 43:7, 9. Each of these texts speak of the LORD dwelling in Zion *forever*. As "the mountain of God," Zion is the place *on earth* where "heaven and earth meet." When Ezekiel hears the LORD say that the place where the Temple is being rebuilt is "the place of the soles of my feet," Ezek 43:7, that is a clear and unmistakable reference to the presence of the LORD *on earth*.[37] The eschatological hope of the Old Testament is contingent upon the eternity of the created world order, i.e., "the heavens and the earth" of Gen 1:1, 2:1.

Psa 96:10 is hardly the only place where the Old Testament alludes to the eternity of creation. The following

---

[36] No Jew in the Old Testament or during time of the New Testament (except perhaps for some, like Philo, who imbibed too much in the dualistic philosophy of Plato) ever expected to die "and go to Heaven" or that the earth would someday be annihilated. Standard Old Testament eschatological hope was for a resurrection to life *on earth*, but an earth radically different than the present earth. The resurrected would eat and drink and engage in various physical activities, Ezek 28:26, 34:13-14. The new earth would be a place of abundance and prosperity, where people would enjoy the fruits of their labor without fear of invasion, Deut 30:9, Ezek 34:28-29. Even nature would be transformed so that animal predation would no longer exist, Isa 11:6-9. The ultimate characterization of this eschatological hope was described as "new heavens and a new earth," Isa 65:17, 66:22.

[37] Let us not forget that earth (in the future) is also the place of the LORD's *throne*, just as in Revelation 22.

texts have been routinely identified in lexicons and theological dictionaries as teaching the eternity of creation:

Psa 78:69
> ⁶⁹He built his sanctuary like the high heavens,
> like the earth, which **he has founded forever**.

Psa 104:5
> ⁵He **set the earth on its foundations,**
> **so that it should never be moved**.

Psa 148:5-6
> ⁵Let them praise the name of the LORD!
> For he commanded and they were created.
> ⁶And **he established them forever and ever;**
> he gave a decree, and **it shall not pass away**.

Eccl 1:4
> ⁴A generation goes, and a generation comes,
> but **the earth remains forever**.³⁸

---

³⁸ The most common Hebrew word for "forever" is ʿôlām. One theological dictionary, after discussing some limitations on the meaning of ʿôlām, goes on to discuss more nuanced meanings including the possibility of it meaning something like our English "forever:"

> In many more cases, the nom. is used with longer time periods in view—indeed, it often implies unceasingness or perpetuity. The nom. is used in this fashion to describe aspects of creation: in Ps 78:69; 104:5; Eccl 1:4, the earth is said to have been established "forever," i.e., it will continue to exist into the most distant future. Similarly, the heavens and their denizens are established forever (Ps 148:6). *Zion, the mountain of God, is also established perpetually* (48:8[9]). NIDOTTE, 3:348, emphasis supplied.

The classic Brown-Driver-Briggs lexicon of Old Testament Hebrew makes a similar semantic distinction in the uses of ʿôlām in Psa 78:69, 104:5, 148:6, and Eccl. 1:4 assigning it the meaning of "continuous existence," BDB, 762, definition 2.b. The older Gesenius lexicon cites Psa 78:69, 104:5, and Eccl 1:4 as conveying "the meta-

The first, Psa 78:69, is interesting for how it relates to Zion's story. Psa 78:53-54 takes us back to the march through the wilderness, and vv. 60, and 67-68, preceding 69, provide further evidence of the context:

> ⁵³He led them in safety, so that they were not afraid,
> but the sea overwhelmed their enemies.
> ⁵⁴And **he brought them to his holy land,**
> **to the mountain** which his right hand had won.³⁹
> ⁶⁰He forsook his dwelling at Shiloh,
> the tent where he dwelt among mankind,
> ⁶⁷He rejected the tent of Joseph;
> he did not choose the tribe of Ephraim,
> ⁶⁸but he chose the tribe of Judah,
> **Mount Zion, which he loves.**
> ⁶⁹He built his **sanctuary** like the high heavens,
> **like the earth, which he has founded forever.**

The earth is a suitable place for Mount Zion, the place "which [the LORD] loves," and where He will "dwell forever," Psa 68:16, 125:1-2, 132:13-17, Ezek 43:7, 9, only because it, too, *will last forever*.

Psa 104:5 is a significant text because it is one of just a few places in the Old Testament where ʿôlām is combined with the Hebrew word ʿaḏ to create an expression that means "forever and ever."⁴⁰ That this is not immediately obvious in Psa 104:5 owes to how the eternity of creation

---

physical idea of eternity, at least as that which has no end . . . *applied to the earth and the whole nature of things.*" Gesenius (1873, DCXIII, A.(2),(c)), emphasis supplied.

³⁹ Note the intertextual echo here of Exod 15:13-18.

⁴⁰ For the use of ʿaḏ with ʿôlām see TWOT, 2: 645, #1565c, Strong's #H7703.

here is stated as a negative. The NASB translation of 104:5 is worth citing completely here to see this:

> ⁵He established the earth upon its foundations,
> So that it will not totter **forever and ever.**

Here is another important Old Testament passage whose significance is hard to overestimate. The Old Testament contains several passages that refer to divine judgment via cosmic disturbances, including judgments upon the whole earth in which the earth "totters," or is "shaken," e.g., Job 9:5-7, Isa 13:13, 34:4, 51:6, Hag 2:6, 21-22, Psa 102:25-26[41]. What Psa 104:5 is saying is that no matter how severe the impact of such disturbances upon the earth, they will never last "forever and ever," they will never last so long as to constitute annihilation of the created world (cosmic) order. This is corroborated by Psa 75:2-3:

> ²"At the set time that I appoint
> I will judge with equity.
> ³When **the earth totters, and all its inhabitants,**
> **it is I who keep steady its pillars.**

The "pillars" of Psa 75:3 are the "foundations" of Psa

---

[41] What is translated "pass away" by the ESV in Psa 102:26 is the Hebrew *ḥālap̄* [Strong's #H2498]. In the Hithpael stem this word is used to signify a change of garments (cf. ESV Gen 35:2) and is so rendered in the NASB (1995) of Psa 102:26:

> ²⁶Even they will perish, but You endure; And all of them will wear out like a garment; Like clothing You will change them and they will be changed.

Cf. KJV, ASV, NKJV; Thayer, 322, 3 (Hiph.); NIDOTTE 2:156, 2. Nothing is implicated here about annihilation.

104:5, upon which God has "established the earth...forever and ever." We should also note here Mic 6:2's reference to the "enduring foundations of the earth." Though God may execute judgment upon the earth with cosmic or cataclysmic results, He will "keep steady its pillars" and not allow it to "totter...forever and ever." It will never *completely* pass away, or be *annihilated*.

We previously saw a connection between the earth being established and never being moved in Psa 96:10:

> [10]*Say **among the nations**, "**The LORD reigns!***
> ***Yes, the world is established; it shall never be moved;***
> *he will **judge the peoples** with equity."*

Behind all of this, that the earth was created to last forever, is that the present *cosmic order* constitutes a "fixed order" that was established in Genesis 1. This "fixed order" is alluded to in Psa 119:89-91:

> [89]***Forever**, O LORD, your word*
> ***is firmly fixed in the heavens.***
> [90]*Your faithfulness **endures to all generations**;*
> *you have **established the earth**, and **it stands fast**.*
> [91]*By your appointment they **stand this day**,*
> *for all things are your servants.*

The Hebrew word translated "established" is often used in contexts related to that which has been "created" and draws attention to the *permanent* nature of what has been "created." According to one lexical resource it has a "nuance of permanence" strengthened here by the grammatical form used.[42] The same source says about the

---

[42] NIDOTTE, 2:616, adding "Because the world is 'established' ... 'it cannot be moved.'" The Hebrew is *kûn* [Strong's H3559].

word translated "stands(s)" in vv. 90-91: "In poetic material," like psalms, "the sense of 'endure' is noticeable."[43] To say that the earth is "established" and "stands fast" to "this day" is testimony to its enduring permanence, that it was established for eternity, even "forever and ever."

The use of 'ôlām and 'aḏ is also found in the third passage that Old Testament lexical resources cite as teaching the eternity of creation, Psa 148:5-6:

> [5]*Let them praise the name of the LORD!*
> *For **he commanded and they were created.***
> [6]*And **he established them forever and ever;***
> *he gave a decree, and **it shall not pass away.***

The "them" in these verses refers to both the spiritual order of that which was created in Gen 1:1 (the angelic host of Heaven) and the material order (the starry heavens). The LORD "commanded and they were created...He established them *forever and ever.*" The "it" of v. 6 refers to the "decree" (that resulted in the creation that "established them forever and ever"). This text is an affirmation of the eternity of God's created cosmic order, both spiritual and material, in Gen 1:1, 2:1, and a scriptural repudiation of any doctrine of eventual annihilation of the earth or the heavens. The heavens and earth will last *forever and ever.*

In Psa 119:89-91 we saw allusions to a "fixed order" of creation. This teaching of a "fixed order" to creation appears in a context important to Zion's story in Psalm 89. Psalm 89 is a meditation upon the covenant God made with David in 2 Samuel 7, especially vv. 12-17. The first 37

---

[43]NIDOTTE, 3: 432. The Hebrew word is 'āmaḏ [Strong's H5975].

verses are a recitation of the promises made to King David and the covenant established by God with David. Verses 38-51 are a lament for what seems to the psalmist a lack of remembrance on God's part of the covenant promises, suggesting a time when it seemed like the promise that a descendant of David would always reign in Zion was threatened. Some think this sets the Psalm during the period of Babylonian captivity. But it is ascribed to "Ethan the Ezrahite" who was a contemporary of David and Solomon. *If* vv. 38-51 reflect conditions during the period of Babylonian captivity, then they are an emendation to the original psalm, and only vv. 1-37 reflect the words of the original psalmist.[44]

What we want to pay attention to here are vv. 24-29 and 34-37:

> [24]*My faithfulness and my steadfast love shall be with him, and in my name shall his horn be exalted.*
> [25]*I will set his hand on the sea*

---

[44] If vv. 38-51 are an emendation to the original psalm, why would those responsible for final canonical form of the book of Psalms have included this emendation? Many have noted how the canonical form of Psalms is divided into 5 "books" (perhaps to be a "Torah" for worship). The first three books express a wide range of emotions – lament, praise, thanksgiving, wisdom, joy, sorrow, struggles, doubts, anger and fear and victories of individuals (like David!). The final two books are more joyful and full of celebration, with a greater sense of confidence and trust in God's covenant faithfulness. Interestingly, Psalm 89 is the *last* psalm in the first three books, and vv. 38-51 may be intended to suggest the kind of negativity that existed at the end of the First Temple period, while books 3 and 4 (chapters 90-150) reflect the more positive view of Israel's eschatological ("messianic") hope of the Second Temple period.

> *and his right hand on the rivers.*[45]
> *^{26}He shall cry to me, 'You are my Father,*
> *my God, and the Rock of my salvation.'*
> *^{27}And I will make him **the firstborn**,*
> ***the highest of the kings of the earth.***[46]
> *^{28}**My steadfast love I will keep for him forever**,*
> *and my covenant **will stand firm for him**.*[47]
> *^{29}I will establish his offspring forever*
> *and his throne as the days of the heavens.*
> *^{34}I will not violate my covenant*
> *or alter the word that went forth from my lips.*
> *^{35}Once for all I have sworn by my holiness;*
> *I will not lie to David.*
> *^{36}**His offspring shall endure forever**,*
> *his throne as long as the sun before me.*
> *^{37} Like the moon it shall be established forever,*
> *a faithful witness in the skies."*

Verses 29, 36, and 37 teach that Messiah will sit on his throne as long as "the days of heaven," as long as the sun and the moon remain "before [Yahweh]...established forever, ...faithful witness[es] in the skies." There is an intertextual echo here of Psa 119:89-91 which links back to the establishment of the luminaries of Gen 1:14, which were to stand as *signs* in the skies. While there are multiple ways in which the sun and the moon might serve as signs,

---

[45] Messiah will be master of the material world order, the created earth.

[46] Vv. 26-27 make clear the messianic focus of the Psalm, pointing to Jesus Christ.

[47] There is classic Hebrew poetic parallelism here in the meanings of "forever" and "stand firm." Cf. the discussion of "stand(s)" on Page 51 and footnote 43.

here the clear sense is that they are "faithful witnesses" to the reliability of God's promises. Just as we can trust the sun and moon to *forever* be signs in the earth's skies, we can trust in the faithfulness and reliability of God's word. Put another way, the earth and the cosmic world order will last as long as God's word can be trusted.

We have an even more explicit appeal from the LORD directly in which He swears by the "fixed order" of the cosmos that His word is sure in Jer 31:35-36:

> ³⁵*Thus says the LORD,*
>   *who gives the sun for light by day*
> *and the fixed order of the moon*
>   *and the stars for light by night,*
> *who **stirs up the sea** so that its waves roar—*
>   *the LORD of hosts is his name:*
> ³⁶*"**If this fixed order departs***
>   *from before me, declares the LORD,*
> ***then shall the offspring of Israel cease***
>   *from being a nation before me **forever**."*

Note how this oath directly follows the promise of a new covenant in Jer 31:31-34, cited in the New Testament in Heb 8:8-12, and therefore the "offspring of Israel" in v. 36 can only refer to those of the new covenant in Christ, the true offspring of Abraham by faith. Yahweh here is swearing by the "fixed order" of the sun, moon, and stars, and by all the evidence of His creative power in nature ("who stirs up the sea so that its waves roar") that what He has just promised in vv. 31-34 is as certain to come pass as is His creation is certain to last forever.⁴⁸ The oath is made

---

⁴⁸ Taken together vv. 31-36 are part of a unit of the book of Jere-

obliquely, but the sense is self-evident. The Old Testament teaches that the earth was created to last forever.

We have covered a lot of ground in this chapter and it is appropriate to recap what we have learned before bringing it to a conclusion. We started the chapter with a quartet of passages affirming the LORD's desire to dwell in Zion *forever*. We then examined Peter's admonition in Acts 3:19-21 to look at what "God spoke by the mouth of his holy prophets long ago" if we are to fully understand what to expect when Jesus comes to "restor[e] all the things about which" they spoke. Psalm 37 provided a good example of how prophets, including David, spoke about things to come, including a promised *inheritance*. While Psalm 37 speaks of this as an inheritance of "the land," we saw that Old Testament prophecy focusing in on what God would accomplish through His "Anointed,"

---

miah, chapters 30-33, often referred to as Jeremiah's "Book of Consolation." This appellation comes from Jer 30:2-3:

> ²*Thus says the LORD, the God of Israel. Write in a book all the words I have spoken to you.* ³**For behold, the days are coming, declares the LORD, when I will restore the fortunes of my people, Israel and Judah**, *says the LORD, and I will bring them back to the land that I gave to their fathers and they shall take possession of it."*

That the focus of this Book of Consolation is eschatological is apparent in the refrain "behold, the days are coming," which occurs in 31:27, 31, 38, and 33:14. The text in 31:27 is notable for it portrays the LORD "sowing" the house of Israel and the house of Judah "with the seed of man and the seed of beast," suggesting that animal life has a place in the age to come, a notion found elsewhere in the Old Testament, cf. Isa 11:6-9, Hos 2:18. Appeal to the "fixed order" of the cosmos as a witness to how the LORD will never break his covenant with David is reprised in 33:19-26, at the end of Jeremiah's Book of Consolation.

the Messiah, enlarged this inheritance to include *all nations* and to extend to *all the earth*.

Which brought us to consider what the Old Testament teaches about the *eternity of the earth*. Contrary to what many think, based on a misunderstanding of New Testament teaching, the earth's destiny is not to be annihilated. It will be judged, and in terms often described as cosmic and cataclysmic. But passages like Psa 75:3 and 104:5 teach that the earth will never so "totter" or undergo such cosmic destruction that it ceases altogether to exist, or is annihilated. God will ensure that the earth will stand firm, and exist forever, that the sun, moon, and stars constitute a "fixed order" that serve as witnesses to the immutability of God's promises concerning a new covenant, and new heavens and a new earth, purged of all unrighteousness, so that the LORD can *return to Zion* and *dwell in the midst of His people forevermore*. In the next chapter, we immerse ourselves in what the Old Testament has to say about "the return to Zion." It is quite a story of its own.

5 THE RETURN TO ZION

There are two different arcs of the "return to Zion" theme in the Old Testament. One deals with passages that refer to the return of Yahweh to Zion. The other deals with texts that refer to the return of the exiles to Zion. The latter are far more numerous and were we to consider them all we would double the length of this book.[49] But that is where we will start, with the return of the exiles, and look at some of the more significant of those texts.

The prophetic witness to an eschatological end-time return of the exiles begins early, in Deut 30:1-10:

> *¹And when all these things come upon you, the blessing and the curse, which I have set before you, and you call them to mind among all the nations where the Lord your God has driven you, ²and return to the Lord your God, you and your children, and obey his voice in all that I command you today, with all your heart and with all your soul,* **³then the Lord your God**

---

[49] There are at least 75 passages in the Psalms and the Prophets that mention the return of the exiles.

*will restore your fortunes and have mercy on you, and he will gather you again from all the peoples where the L*ORD *your God has scattered you. ⁴If your outcasts are in the uttermost parts of heaven, from there the L*ORD *your God will gather you, and from there he will take you. ⁵And the L*ORD *your God will bring you into the land that your fathers possessed, that you may possess it. And he will make you more prosperous and numerous than your fathers. ⁶And the L*ORD *your God will circumcise your heart and the heart of your offspring, so that you will love the L*ORD *your God with all your heart and with all your soul, that you may live. ⁷And the L*ORD *your God will put all these curses on your foes and enemies who persecuted you. ⁸And you shall again obey the voice of the L*ORD *and keep all his commandments that I command you today. ⁹The L*ORD *your God will make you abundantly prosperous in all the work of your hand, in the fruit of your womb and in the fruit of your cattle and in the fruit of your ground. For the L*ORD *will again take delight in prospering you, as he took delight in your fathers, ¹⁰when you obey the voice of the L*ORD *your God, to keep his commandments and his statutes that are written in this Book of the Law, when you turn to the L*ORD *your God with all your heart and with all your soul.*

The first thing to make clear is that return of the exiles "into the land that your fathers possessed" has nothing to do with the return from Babylonian captivity. The return from Babylonian captivity was never more than a *limited* return of exiles, and not even all the exiles in Babylon chose to return.[50] This prophecy in Deuteronomy 30 is of a *universal* return from exile. As we will see shortly

---

[50] Cf. the previous remarks on pp. 39-40 and footnote 53.

many of these texts will explicitly depict the universal nature of this return from exile by specifically mentioning both Judah and Israel.[51]

---

[51] I would remind the reader here of the significance of the end-time reunification of Israel and Judah discussed previously on pp. 16-18. This is a figure of the union of Jew and Greek as one new humanity in Christ Jesus. Some think they see a dual-fulfillment or typological interpretation in Deut 30:1-10 and subsequent prophecies of a restored Davidic monarchy reuniting Israel and Judah and the end-time return of the exiles to Zion that would allow for partial fulfillment in the return from Babylonian captivity. I do not deny the existence of dual-fulfillment and typological texts, but I do not see them here. Two examples that come readily to mind are 2 Sam 7:12-15 (which had an initial application to David's immediate offspring, and an eventual application to Christ), or Isa 7:14 (which had an initial fulfillment in Isaiah's day, but eventually applied to the birth of Jesus). But in each of these examples, the near-term fulfillment is detailed with specifics. Nothing in Deut 30:1-10 or later prophecies like Ezek 37:15-28 specifically relate to the return from Babylonian captivity. Some may think they see this in Deut 30:5. But this same kind of "return to the land" language is found in Ezek 37:24-28 where it is clearly and unmistakably referring to a "land" (a "heritage" or "inheritance") for those living under the reign of the Messiah, and therefore *cannot* refer to the return from Babylonian captivity. The sense of Deut 30:5 is surely the same.

As for a typological application of the return from Babylonian captivity, I would point to Jer 29:10-14. On the near-term fulfillment in the return from Babylonian captivity, the details of vv. 10-11 are clear and unmistakable. I view verse 12 as transitional, especially considering Daniel 9 and all the prayers likely offered throughout the intertestamental period for fulfillment of Isa 40:1-11, cf. Luke 2:25-32. Verse 13 echoes Deut 30:6, Ezek 11:19, 36:26, 27, et al. and verse 14 completes the segue to the end-time return of the exiles the latter days. Here I would have no problem describing the return from Babylonian captivity as a *type* of the ultimate end-time return of the redeemed in Christ. But the kind of details that warrant that here are lacking in Deut 30:1-10, Ezek 37:15-28, and similar prophecies that are wholly messianic and eschatological, and should not be read into them.

A second thing to note is the "circumcision of the heart" in v. 6. That links this text with texts in Jeremiah and Ezekiel, e.g., Jer 31:33, 32:39-40, Ezek 11:19, 36:26-27, where God promises to give His covenant faithful a "new heart" and "a new spirit." Paul uses language from Jer 31:33 and Ezek 11:19 in 2 Cor 3:3 in an allusion to the indwelling of the Holy Spirit:

> *³And you show that you are a letter from Christ delivered by us, **written not with ink but with the Spirit of the living God, not on tablets of stone but on tablets of human hearts.***

Turning to the Prophets, and starting with Isaiah, noteworthy texts regarding the return of the exiles include:

Isa 11:11-12
> *¹¹In that day the L*ORD *will extend his hand yet a second time **to recover the remnant** that remains of his people, from Assyria, from Egypt, from Pathros, from Cush, from Elam, from Shinar, from Hamath, and from **the coastlands of the sea.***
> *¹²He will raise a signal for the nations*
> *and **will assemble the banished of Israel,***
> *and **gather the dispersed of Judah***
> *from **the four corners of the earth.***

Isa 35:10
> *¹⁰And **the ransomed of the L*ORD *shall return***
> *and **come to Zion with singing;***
> *everlasting joy shall be upon their heads;*
> *they shall obtain gladness and joy,*
> *and sorrow and sighing shall flee away.*

Isa 56:6-8
> *⁶"And **the foreigners who join themselves to the L*ORD*,***
> *to minister to him, to love the name of the L*ORD*,*

and to be his servants,
>   everyone who keeps the Sabbath and does not
> profane it, and holds fast my covenant—
> ⁷**these I will bring to my holy mountain,**
>   **and make them joyful in my house of prayer;**
> their burnt offerings and their sacrifices
>   will be accepted on my altar;
> for my house shall be called a house of prayer
>   **for all peoples."**
> ⁸The Lord God,
>   **who gathers the outcasts of Israel, declares,**
> **"I will gather yet others to him**
>   **besides those already gathered."**

Isa 66:18-20

> ¹⁸"For I know their works and their thoughts, **and the time is coming to gather all nations and tongues. And they shall come and shall see my glory,** ¹⁹and I will set a sign among them. And from them I will send survivors to the nations, to Tarshish, Pul, and Lud, who draw the bow, to Tubal and Javan, **to the coastlands far away,** that have not heard my fame or seen my glory. And they shall declare my glory among the nations. ²⁰**And they shall bring all your brothers from all the nations as an offering to the Lord,** on horses and in chariots and in litters and on mules and on dromedaries, **to my holy mountain Jerusalem,** says the Lord, just as the Israelites bring their grain offering in a clean vessel to the house of the Lord. [52]

That we have here in these passages from Isaiah a univer-

---

[52] The "coastlands" frequently noted in these "return of the exiles" texts are the lands around the coast of the Mediterranean, and reflect the "world-wide" dispersion of exiles being called back, not just the exiles in Babylon.

sal end-time ingathering and not the return from Babylonian captivity (cf. footnote 51) should be obvious. In 11:11-12 a remnant from *both* Judah and Israel is brought back from multiple nations, not just Babylon. In 35:10 (which is repeated in Isa 51:11) the destiny is Zion, not Heaven. The universal scope of this ingathering is extended to foreigners, and is for all peoples and not just the outcasts of Israel, 56:6-8, and their destiny is the holy mount (Zion). The universal scope is also emphasized in 66:18-20, where people from all nations and tongues will come to the LORD's holy mountain in Jerusalem.[53]

Passages from Jeremiah which foretell of a universal end-time ingathering include:

Jer 23:3-4
> *³Then **I will gather the remnant of my flock out of all the countries where I have driven them, and I will bring them back to their fold**, and they shall be fruitful and multiply. ⁴I will set shepherds over them who will care for them, and they shall fear no more, nor be dismayed, neither shall any be missing, declares the LORD.*

Jer 29:14
> *¹⁴I will be found by you, declares the LORD, and I will*

---

[53] Some have sought to limit the meaning of "new heavens and new earth" in Isa 65:17 and 66:22 calling it a figure for the return from Babylonian captivity. Among other persuasive arguments against this view is how it totally ignores the clear context of Isaiah 65 and 66. Especially in Isaiah 66 (and exactly like 2 Pet 3:13 and Rev 21:1), the image of "new heavens and new earth" appears in a context of *final judgment*, vv. 15-24. Note especially v. 23b, which directly follows the reference to "new heavens and new earth" in v. 22: "*all flesh* [of those not affected by the fiery judgment of vv. 16 and 24] shall come to worship me," e.g., not just the few who returned from Babylon in the 6th century before Christ.

restore your fortunes and gather you from all the nations and all the places where I have driven you, declares the LORD, and *I will bring you back to the place from which I sent you into exile.*

Jer 31:8a, 10-12

⁸Behold, I will bring them from the north country
and gather them from the farthest parts of the earth,

¹⁰"Hear the word of the LORD, O nations,
and *declare it in the coastlands far away;*
say, *'He who scattered Israel will gather him,*
and will keep him as a shepherd keeps his flock.'
¹¹For *the LORD has ransomed Jacob*
and has redeemed him from hands too strong for him.
¹²*They shall come and sing aloud on the height of Zion,*
and they shall be radiant over the goodness
of the LORD,
over the grain, the wine, and the oil,
and over the young of the flock and the herd;
their life shall be like a watered garden,
and they shall languish no more.

Jer 32:37-41

³⁷*Behold, I will gather them from all the countries to which I drove them* in my anger and my wrath and in great indignation. *I will bring them back to this place, and I will make them dwell in safety.* ³⁸*And they shall be my people, and I will be their God.* ³⁹*I will give them one heart* and one way, that they may fear me forever, for their own good and the good of their children after them. ⁴⁰*I will make with them an everlasting covenant,* that I will not turn away from doing good to them. And I will put the fear of me in their hearts, that they may not turn from me. ⁴¹I will rejoice in doing them good, *and I will plant them in this land in faithfulness,* with all my heart and all my soul.

Note in 29:14 the promise to "restore your fortunes" and to "bring you back." The promise to "restore your fortunes" echoes Deut 30:3. The promise to be "brought back" has no figurative significance to the idea of eternity in Heaven, since that is not a place we have ever been to in this life. It does, however, have figurative significance to being restored to a radically renewed *earth*.

In Psa 115:16 we are told:

> ¹⁶*The heavens are the LORD's heavens,*
> **but the earth he has given to the children of man.**

When God created the heavens and the earth in Genesis 1, He intended for it to be an *eternal* habitation for humanity. God's original plan and purpose was never for humanity to die and join Him forevermore in Heaven. Had Adam fulfilled the creation mandate of Gen 1:26-28, Adam's offspring would have gone out into all the earth bearing God's image such that the glory of God would have filled the earth, cf. Num 14:21, Psa 72:19, Isa 11:9, Hab 2:14, turning the entire earth into a holy temple of the LORD. What we see in Revelation 21-22 is something comparable, a new Jerusalem filled with God's people coming "back" to earth, a radically renewed earth, filled with the glory of the LORD. What is being depicted in the Old Testament prophecies of a return to Zion and a return to "the land" prefigures a restoration and return of a redeemed humanity to a new earth that has now become Zion and God's holy mountain.

Ezekiel, too, has its share of texts of the universal end-time ingathering of the redeemed:

Ezek 11:17, 19-20
¹⁷*Therefore say, 'Thus says the Lord GOD:* **I will gather**

you from the peoples and **assemble you out of the countries where you have been scattered,** *and I will give you the land of Israel.'*

[19]*And I will give them one heart, and a new spirit I will put within them.* *I will remove the heart of stone from their flesh and give them a heart of flesh,* [20] *that they may walk in my statutes and keep my rules and obey them.* **And they shall be my people, and I will be their God.**

Ezek 28:25-26

[25]*"Thus says the Lord GOD:* **When I gather the house of Israel from the peoples among whom they are scattered,** *and manifest my holiness in them in the sight of the nations,* **then they shall dwell in their own land** *that I gave to my servant Jacob.* [26]**And they shall dwell securely in it,** *and they shall build houses and plant vineyards. They shall dwell securely, when I execute judgments upon all their neighbors who have treated them with contempt.* **Then they will know that I am the LORD their God."**

Ezek 34:13-14, 25-26, 29-31

[13]*And* **I will bring them out from the peoples and gather them from the countries, and will bring them into their own land. And I will feed them on the mountains of Israel,** *by the ravines,* **and in all the inhabited places of the country.** [14]*I will feed them with good pasture, and on the mountain heights of Israel shall be their grazing land. There they shall lie down in good grazing land,* **and on rich pasture they shall feed on the mountains of Israel.**

[25]**"I will make with them a covenant of peace and banish wild beasts from the land, so that they may dwell securely in the wilderness and sleep in the woods.** [26]*And I will make them and the places all around my*

*hill a blessing, and **I will send down the showers in their season; they shall be showers of blessing.***

*²⁹**And I will provide for them renowned plantations so that they shall no more be consumed with hunger in the land,** and no longer suffer the reproach of the nations.* *³⁰**And they shall know that I am the Lord their God with them,** and that they, the house of Israel, are my people, declares the Lord God.* *³¹**And you are my sheep, human sheep of my pasture, and I am your God,** declares the Lord God."*

Ezek 37:21-22

*²¹then say to them, Thus says the Lord God: Behold, **I will take the people of Israel from the nations among which they have gone, and will gather them from all around, and bring them to their own land.** ²²**And I will make them one nation in the land, on the mountains of Israel.** And one king shall be king over them all, **and they shall be no longer two nations, and no longer divided into two kingdoms.***

Ezek 39:25, 28-29

*²⁵ "Therefore thus says the Lord God: Now **I will restore the fortunes of Jacob and have mercy on the whole house of Israel,** and I will be jealous for my holy name.*

*²⁸**Then they shall know that I am the Lord their God, because I sent them into exile among the nations and then assembled them into their own land.** I will leave none of them **remaining among the nations anymore.** ²⁹And I will not hide my face anymore from them, **when I pour out my Spirit** upon the house of Israel, declares the Lord God."*

One thing notable in these passages from Ezekiel is how often the return to "the land" is described by felicitous earthly delights. To generations of Christians taught that eternity will be some kind of ethereal and purely spiritual affair, often caricaturized with the image of saints floating on clouds strumming harps (signifying an eternity focused entirely on praise and worship of God and the Lamb), to suggest that these images of felicitous earthly welfare are a more accurate depiction of eternity may be hard to grasp. Now, there is certainly an element of figurative language in this depiction of life on earth in the age to come. For instance, "the land" is no longer the literal land along the Jordan, or even the land from Egypt to the Euphrates that Solomon ruled over, but is a "land" that now encompasses all nations, peoples, and the whole earth. This is how it is viewed in the New Testament in passages like Matt 5:5 and Rom 4:13:

Matt 5:5
> [5]"*Blessed are the meek, for they shall **inherit the earth**.*"[54]

Rom 4:13
> [13]*For the promise to Abraham and his offspring that he would **inherit the world** did not come through the law but through the righteousness of faith.*[55]

In other words, "the land of promise" for eternity has become the "new heavens and new earth." Other depictions must certainly allow for some degree of figurativeness. To "dwell securely" is depicted as being free from

---

[54] Jesus is drawing on Psalm 37 here. The reader may wish to revisit the discussion of Psalm 37 above (pp. 37-40) and the discussion that followed (pp. 40-43) showing how even in the Old Testament the eschatological hope anticipated a rule by the LORD's Anointed (Messiah) that would encompass the whole earth.

[55] I have substituted the NET Bible's "inherit" for the ESV's "be heir of."

fear of wild beasts (or in other passages, invasion). Prosperity is depicted as being free from hunger and enjoying enhanced agricultural productivity. Since the redeemed will encompass saints from every age of material progress, there is no way to know how this will be accounted for in the age to come. I do believe that the age to come will involve varying levels and kinds of human activity consistent with life on a new *earth*. But to say much more would soon involve rank speculation.

For a few examples from the Minor Prophets, we have:

Amos 9:13-15
> [13]*"Behold, the days are coming,"* declares the L<small>ORD</small>,
>   *"when the plowman shall overtake the reaper*
>   *and the treader of grapes him who sows the seed;*
>   ***the mountains shall drip sweet wine,***
>   ***and all the hills shall flow with it.***
> [14]*I will **restore the fortunes** of my people Israel,*
>   *and they shall rebuild the ruined*
>   *cities and inhabit them;*
>   *they shall plant vineyards and drink their wine,*
>   *and they shall make gardens and eat their fruit.*
> [15]***I will plant them on their land,***
>   *and they shall never again be uprooted*
> *out of the land that I have given them,"*
>   *says the L<small>ORD</small> your God.*

Mic 4:6-7
> [6]*In that day, declares the L<small>ORD</small>,*
>   *I will assemble the lame*
>   ***and gather those who have been driven away***
>   *and those whom I have afflicted;*
> [7]*and the lame **I will make the remnant,***
>   ***and those who were cast off, a strong nation;***
>   ***and the L<small>ORD</small> will reign over them in Mount Zion***

> *from this time forth and forevermore.*

Zeph 3:18-20
> *[18] I will gather those of you who mourn for the festival,*
> > *so that you will no longer suffer reproach.*
> *[19] Behold, at that time I will deal*
> > *with all your oppressors.*
> *And I will save the lame*
> > *and gather the outcast,*
> *and I will change their shame into praise*
> > *and renown in all the earth.*
> *[20] At that time I will bring you in,*
> > *at the time when I gather you together;*
> *for I will make you renowned and praised*
> > *among all the **peoples of the earth**,*
> *when I **restore your fortunes***
> > *before your eyes," says the* LORD.

Zech 8:7-8, 10:8-10
> *[7] Thus says the* LORD *of hosts: Behold, **I will save my people from the east country and from the west country**, [8] and **I will bring them** to dwell **in the midst of Jerusalem**. And **they shall be my people, and I will be their God**, in faithfulness and in righteousness."*

> *[8] "I will whistle for them and **gather them in**,*
> > *for I have redeemed them,*
> *and they shall be as many as they were before.*
> *[9] Though I scattered them among the nations,*
> > *yet in far countries they shall remember me,*
> *and with their children **they shall live and return**.*
> *[10] I will **bring them home** from the land of Egypt,*
> > *and gather them from Assyria,*
> *and **I will bring them** to the land of Gilead*
> > *and to Lebanon, till there is no room for them.*

If all of this seems like a lot of repetition, consider that an indication of how important it is, that this was all written *for our sake*. Though written in a way that seemed to apply to God's people in the Old Testament, according to what Peter says in Acts 3:21 these are things that pertain to what is to happen *in our future* when Jesus returns. *We* will be among the ransomed who will be gathered from among all nations and return to Zion with singing. *We* will settle in the land of promise that is the ultimate inheritance of Abraham's offspring, Zion, the mountain of God, and the new Jerusalem. *Our* destiny is joined to the renewal of creation, that God might fulfill His desire to dwell in the midst of His creation and receive the praises of its glory. These Old Testament promises warrant our study and meditation if we are to properly comprehend the work of reconciliation that God is accomplishing in Christ. As Paul put it in 2 Cor 1:20, "***All*** of God's promises find their Yes in Him [Christ]." Including all the promises about the "return to Zion."

So far, we have focused on the first of the two arcs identified at the beginning of this chapter, the return of the exiles (and the pilgrimage of the nations) to Zion in the last day. Now we turn to the second arc, the LORD's return to Zion. A fit start is two of the quartet of passages we considered earlier about God desiring to dwell in Zion forever:

Psa 132:13-17
>^{13}*For **the LORD has chosen Zion;**
>   **he has desired it for his dwelling place:***
>^{14}*"**This is my resting place forever;**
>   **here I will dwell, for I have desired it.***
>^{15}*I will abundantly bless her provisions;
>   I will satisfy her poor with bread.*
>^{16}*Her priests I will clothe with salvation,*

> *and her saints will shout for joy.*
> *¹⁷There I will make a horn to sprout for David;*
> *I have prepared a lamp for my anointed.*

Ezek 43:7, 9

> *⁷and he said to me, "Son of man, this is the place of my throne and the place of the soles of my feet, where **I will dwell in the midst of the people of Israel forever**. And the house of Israel shall no more defile my holy name, neither they, nor their kings, by their whoring and by the dead bodies of their kings at their high places,... ⁹Now let them put away their whoring and the dead bodies of their kings far from me, and **I will dwell in their midst forever**.*

Yahweh has chosen Zion to be the place where He will dwell in the midst of the people of Israel forever. Not Heaven, but Zion.[56] As noted previously, Ezekiel 10-11 records Ezekiel's vision of Yahweh departing the Temple prior to the destruction of Jerusalem and the Temple by

---

[56] Does Rev 14:1-5, with the 144,000 standing on Mount Zion, suggest that the New Testament has "spiritualized" the Zion motif and that Mount Zion is now "in Heaven?" That oversimplifies the significance of the text, which has both "now" and "not yet" aspects to it. The "now" is in the depiction of those who have been "redeemed from the earth" (v. 3) during the intermediate state. So, it can be said that Mount Zion as the place where disembodied saints rest in the presence of God is *now* in Heaven, but that there is a *not yet* where at the end of the age Zion comes down "out of Heaven" to the new earth, Rev 3:12, 21:2, 10, as the place where God will *then* dwell in the midst of His people forever. The "now" perspective is reflected in New Testament texts, based on Old Testament prophecy, such as Acts 2:17-39 (Joel 2:32), Acts 13:33, Heb 1:5, 5:5 (Psa 2:6-7), cf. Heb 12:22-24. Besides the obvious significance of the "out of Heaven" passages in Revelation, the "not yet" perspective is evident from the numerous Old Testament passages depicting an end-time *return* of the LORD to Zion under discussion here.

the Babylonians in 587 BC. If Yahweh is to dwell in the midst of His people forever, He must at some point "return to Zion." While not as frequent as texts promising the return of the exiles, there are still several clear and notable texts promising the LORD's return to Zion.

Consider Isa 52:7-9:

> *⁷How beautiful upon the mountains*
> *are the feet of him who brings good news,*
> *who publishes peace, who brings good news*
> *of happiness, who publishes salvation,*
> *who says to Zion, "Your God reigns."*
> *⁸The voice of your watchmen—they lift up their voice;*
> *together they sing for joy;*
> *for eye to eye they see*
> *the return of the LORD to Zion.*
> *⁹Break forth together into singing,*
> *you waste places of Jerusalem,*
> *for the LORD has comforted his people;*
> *he has redeemed Jerusalem.*
> *¹⁰The LORD has bared his holy arm*
> *before the eyes of all the nations,*
> *and all the ends of the earth shall see*
> *the salvation of our God.*

This text is a classic example of what Old Testament scholars refer to as "prophetic foreshortening." The term refers to how, from the standpoint of Old Testament prophecy, Israel's eschatological hope viewed the coming of God and His Messiah as a singular event at the end of the age, whereas we know from our perspective as citizens of the New Testament that there will be *two* comings of Christ, and that the "last days" will be a protracted time period.

Verse 7 is quoted by Paul in Rom 10:15. The preaching of the gospel has *already* inaugurated the Kingdom of God in the last days, Acts 2:17, and may be viewed as the *beginning* of the ingathering of the exiles and of the pilgrimage of the nations promised in the Old Testament. But the ultimate consummation of the promised coming of God and His Anointed, Jesus the Messiah, has *not yet* taken place. Those who have *already* "come to Zion" in a spiritual sense, Heb 12:22-24,[57] and are anxiously awaiting and hastening the coming of new heavens and a new earth as a new cosmic material order, 2 Pet 3:13, are like the "watchmen" of verse 8.

The return of the LORD to Zion is depicted as a "Redeemer" coming in both judgment and salvation, in the final verses of Isaiah 59 and the opening verses of chapter 60, 59:18-21 to 60:3:

> [18]*According to their deeds, so will he repay,*
> *wrath to his adversaries, repayment to his enemies;*
> *to the coastlands he will render repayment.*
> [19]*So they shall fear the name of the LORD from the west,*
> *and his glory from the rising of the sun;*
> ***for he will come*** *like a rushing stream,*
> *which the wind of the LORD drives.*
> [20]***"And a Redeemer will come to Zion,***
> *to those in Jacob who turn from transgression,"*
> *declares the LORD.*
> [21]*"And as for me, this is* ***my covenant*** *with them,"*
> *says the LORD: "****My Spirit that is upon you****, and my*

---

[57] This text, and its "not yet" significance, as well as the "prophetic foreshortening" mentioned in the preceding paragraph, are discussed further in the next chapter in relation to Old Testament texts showing Zion and the returning exiles under attack from hostile forces.

> words that I have put in your mouth, shall not depart out of your mouth, or out of the mouth of your offspring, or out of the mouth of your children's offspring," says the LORD, **"from this time forth and forevermore."**
>
> ¹*Arise, shine, for your light has come,*
> *and the glory of the LORD has risen upon you.*[58]
> ²*For behold, darkness shall cover the earth,*
> *and thick darkness the peoples;*
> **but the LORD will arise upon you,**
> **and his glory will be seen upon you.**
> ³*And* **nations shall come to your light,**
> **and kings to the brightness of your rising.**

That these verses are messianic, and have their "Yes" (2 Cor 1:20) in the two comings of Christ, and not to any provenance in the return from Babylonian captivity, should be self-evident. The new covenant and outpouring of the Spirit of Yahweh have *already* been realized in Messiah's first coming. Verses 1-3 of chapter 60 are *being* fulfilled now, and will be *completely* fulfilled at Jesus' second coming.

That what is being depicted in vv. 1-3 is a return to Zion, *on earth*, is made clear in 60:10-14:

> ¹⁰*Foreigners shall build up your walls,*
> *and their kings shall minister to you;*
> *for in my wrath I struck you,*
> *but in my favor I have had mercy on you.*
> ¹¹**Your gates shall be open continually;**
> **day and night they shall not be shut,**
> **that people may bring to you the wealth of the nations,**

---

[58] Isa 60:1 is cited by Paul in Eph 5:14 where he ascribes "the glory of the LORD" to Jesus, as part of a now/not yet application of this text.

> with their kings led in procession.
> ¹²For the nation and kingdom
> > that will not serve you shall perish;
> > those nations shall be utterly laid waste.
> ¹³The glory of Lebanon shall come to you,
> > the cypress, the plane, and the pine,
> > **to beautify the place of my sanctuary,**
> > **and I will make the place of my feet glorious.**
> ¹⁴The sons of those who afflicted you
> > shall come bending low to you,
> > and all who despised you
> > shall bow down at your feet;
> > **they shall call you the City of the LORD,**
> > **the Zion of the Holy One of Israel.**

That the "City of the LORD" and "the Zion of the Holy One of Israel" is the new Jerusalem of Revelation 21-22 is clear from the allusion to 60:11 in Rev 21:25-26. That the new Jerusalem is an *earthly* sanctuary is made clear in the second refrain of v. 13, "to beautify the place of my sanctuary, and I will *make the place of my feet glorious*" (cf. Ezek 43:7)." Heaven is never described as the place of God's feet; this is a clear reference to *earth* as the sanctuary of God in the age to come.

Some of the strongest language about Yahweh's return to Zion is found in Zechariah:

Zech 2:10-12
> ¹⁰*Sing and rejoice, O Daughter Zion,*[59] *for behold, I am coming*[60] *and I will dwell in your midst, declares*

---

[59] Following the NIV and NRSV, I have substituted "Daughter Zion" for the ESV's "daughter of Zion." The NET Bible has "Zion my Daughter."

[60] Following the NASB, NIV, and several other translations, I have substituted "I am coming" for the ESV's "I come." The underlying

the LORD. ¹¹*And **many nations shall join themselves to the LORD in that day, and shall be my people. And I will dwell in your midst,** and you shall know that the LORD of hosts has sent me to you.* ¹²*And **the LORD will inherit Judah as his portion in the holy land, and will again choose Jerusalem.**"*

Zech 8:3, 7-8, 20-23

³*Thus says the LORD: **I have returned to Zion and will dwell in the midst of Jerusalem,** and Jerusalem shall be called the faithful city, and **the mountain of the LORD of hosts, the holy mountain.***

⁷*Thus says the LORD of hosts: Behold, **I will save my people from the east country and from the west country,*** ⁸*and I will bring them **to dwell in the midst of Jerusalem. And they shall be my people, and I will be their God,** in faithfulness and in righteousness."*

²⁰*"Thus says the LORD of hosts: **Peoples shall yet come,** even the inhabitants of many cities.* ²¹*The inhabitants of one city shall go to another, saying, 'Let us go at once to entreat the favor of the LORD and to seek the LORD of hosts; I myself am going.'* ²²***Many peoples and strong nations shall come to seek the LORD of hosts in Jerusalem and to entreat the favor of the LORD.**²³ *Thus says the LORD of hosts: In those days ten **men from the nations of every tongue** shall take hold of the robe of a Jew, saying, 'Let us go with you, for we have heard that God is with you.'"*

The "I have returned to Zion" in 8:3 is a "prophetic present," a verbal figure of speech in which that which is yet to come is so certain that it is rendered in the present

---

Hebrew is a participle describing the action of the verb that follows ("to dwell") and is not a separate verb with its own action as the ESV's translation implies.

tense.[61] It is clear from the overall context that this is prophecy, not something that had already occurred in Zechariah's time. Verses 7 and 8 of chapter 8 describe the end-time ingathering of the exiles, and vv. 20-23 the accompanying end-time pilgrimage of the nations to Zion. As has been previously suggested, there may be a now/not yet aspect to this from a New Testament perspective, i.e., that the ingathering of the exiles and the pilgrimage of the nations has already (now) begun with the preaching of the gospel, but eventually (not yet) this age will come to an end with the final coming of Yahweh and His Anointed as depicted in Revelation 21-22.

---

[61] The actual tense of the Hebrew is the perfect tense, implying completed action.

ZION'S STORY

6 ZION – THE END GAME

There is considerable similarity in the many Old Testament texts considered in the previous chapter of an end-time ingathering of the exiles to Zion. But in some cases, there are prophecies of hostile nations attacking Zion after the exiles have returned to Zion. We will look briefly at some of those prophecies in this chapter and consider how this might impact how we understand our eschatological hope from a New Testament perspective.

A good example of this motif of hostile nations attacking the exiles that have come to Zion is found in Ezekiel. In Ezekiel chapters 34-37 we have multiple depictions of Israel's eschatological hope such as in the texts we looked at on pp. 65-66 (34:13-14, 25-26, 29-31, 37:21-22). And in chapters 40-47 we have Ezekiel's vision of the eschatological temple where God will dwell in the midst of His people forevermore. But *between* chapters 34-37 and 40-47 are chapters 38-39 detailing an end-time apocalyptic battle with Gog and Magog. Gog, the leader of tribes in the land of Magog, is depicted as leading a coalition of hostile nations (Persia, Cush, Put, Gomer, and others) against God's people in Zion. That this is portrayed as happening *after* the exiles have returned to Zion is clear from Ezek 38:7-9:

> [7]"Be ready and keep ready, you and all your hosts that are assembled about you, and be a guard for them. [8]After many days you will be mustered. **In the latter years you will go against the land that is restored from war, the land whose people were gathered from many peoples upon the mountains of Israel, which had been a continual waste. Its people were brought out from the peoples and now dwell securely, all of them.** [9]You will advance, coming on like a storm. You will be like a cloud covering the land, you and all your hordes, and many peoples with you.

A few verses later, 14-16:

> [14]"Therefore, son of man, prophesy, and say to Gog, Thus says the Lord GOD: **On that day when my people Israel are dwelling securely,** will you not know it? [15]You will come from your place out of the uttermost parts of the north, you and many peoples with you, all of them riding on horses, a great host, a mighty army. [16] **You will come up against my people Israel, like a cloud covering the land. In the latter days I will bring you against my land, that the nations may know me, when through you, O Gog, I vindicate my holiness before their eyes.**

Eventually, in the rest of chapter 38, and then in 39, we learn that the LORD allowed this attack on Zion so that the nations "shall know that I am the LORD, the Holy One in Israel," 39:7b. The attack fails, and the forces of Gog are depicted as being defeated, their carcasses eaten by birds and beasts of every sort in what is described as "a great sacrificial feast on the mountains of Israel," 39:17.[62] Chapter 39 ends on a note of victory, vv. 25-29:

> [25]"Therefore thus says the Lord GOD: Now **I will restore the fortunes** of Jacob and have mercy on the whole house of Israel, and I will be jealous for my holy name. [26]They shall forget their shame and all the treachery they have practiced against me, when **they dwell securely in their land** with none to make them afraid, [2] **when I have brought them back from the peoples and gathered them from their enemies' lands**, and through them have vindicated my holiness in the sight of many nations. [28]Then they shall know that I am the LORD their God, because I sent them into exile among the nations and then assembled them into their own land. I will leave none of them remaining among the nations anymore. [29] And **I will not hide my face anymore from them, when I pour out my Spirit upon the house of Israel**, declares the Lord GOD."

What is going on here? Already, back in chapter 34, vv. 11-16, Israel has been promised rescue and salvation when brought back to "their own land" (v. 13) and a covenant of peace in which "they may dwell securely," vv. 25-28. How are we to understand this in light of Zion being attacked in Chapters 38-39? I think the New Testament sheds light on this, but before we look at what the New Testament says, we will look at two more examples of this Old Testament portrayal of eschatological hope associated with attacks by hostile nations.

---

[62] Cf. the "great supper of God," Rev 19:17-21.

Zechariah chapters 9-14 portray a similar pattern of eschatological hope mixed with end-time apocalyptic hostility and warfare. An ingathering of exiles from both "the house of Judah" and "the house of Joseph" is promised in chapter 10, vv. 6-12. But in 12:9 and 14:1-3 we see Jerusalem under attack by hostile nations. Then in 14:5b-9 we have a vision of final victory like we might find in the last book of the New Testament:

> 5b*Then* **the LORD my God will come, and all the holy ones with him.**
> 6 **On that day** *there shall be no light, cold, or frost.*
> 7*And there shall be a unique day, which is known to the LORD, neither day nor night, but at evening time there shall be light.*[63]
> 8 **On that day** *living waters shall flow out from Jerusalem, half of them to the eastern sea and half of them to the western sea. It shall continue in summer as in winter.*[64]
> 9 **And the LORD will be king over all the earth.**[65] *On that day the LORD will be one and his name one.*

Similarly, in Joel 3 we have an end-time apocalyptic judgment of the nations following the restoration of the fortunes of Judah and Jerusalem, 3:1-2, 11-12, 15-17, 20-21:

> 1*For behold,* **in those days and at that time, when I restore the fortunes of Judah and Jerusalem,** 2*I will* **gather all the nations** *and bring them down to the*

---

[63] Cf. Rev 21:23, 25, 22:5, Isa 60:19-20.
[64] Rivers flow from the throne or the temple of the end-time Jerusalem in Ezek 47:1ff, Joel 3:18, Rev 22:1, cf. Psa 46:4, Isa 33:21.
[65] Note how the end-time reign from the eschatological Jerusalem is over "all the earth," not "in Heaven."

> *Valley of Jehoshaphat. And I will enter **into judgment with them** there, **on behalf of my people** and my heritage Israel, **because they have scattered them among the nations and have divided up my land**,*
>
> ¹¹*Hasten and come,*
>   *all you surrounding nations,*
>   *and gather yourselves there.*
>   *Bring down your warriors, O Lord.*
> ¹²*Let the nations stir themselves up*
>   *and come up to the Valley of Jehoshaphat;*
> **for there I will sit to judge**
> **all the surrounding nations.**
>
> ¹⁵*The sun and the moon are darkened,*
>   *and the stars withdraw their shining.*
> ¹⁶**The Lord roars from Zion,**
>   **and utters his voice from Jerusalem,**
>   *and the heavens and the earth quake.*
> **But the Lord is a refuge to his people,**
> **a stronghold to the people of Israel.**
> ¹⁷*"So you shall know that I am the Lord your God,*
>   *who **dwells in Zion, my holy mountain**.*
> **And Jerusalem shall be holy,**
>   **and strangers shall never again pass through it.**
> ²⁰*But **Judah shall be inhabited forever**,*
>   **and Jerusalem to all generations.**
> ²¹*I will avenge their blood,*
>   *blood I have not avenged,*
> **for the Lord dwells in Zion."**

Joel provides us a way forward to understand these prophecies of attacks on Zion depicted after exiles have been restored to the land from a New Testament perspective on eschatology. The final verses of Joel chapter 2, vv. 28-32, were quoted by Peter on the Day of Pentecost in Acts 2:

> ²⁸ *"And it shall come to pass afterward,*
>   *that **I will pour out my Spirit on all flesh**;*
> *your sons and your daughters shall prophesy,*
>   *your old men shall dream dreams,*
> *and your young men shall see visions.*
> ²⁹ *Even on the male and female servants*
>   *in those days I will pour out my Spirit.*
> ³⁰ *"And I will show wonders in the heavens and on the earth, blood and fire and columns of smoke.* ³¹ *The sun shall be turned to darkness, and the moon to blood, before the great and awesome day of the* LORD *comes.* ³² *And it shall come to pass **that everyone who calls on the name of the** LORD **shall be saved. For in Mount Zion and in Jerusalem** there shall be those who escape, as the* LORD *has said, and among the survivors **shall be those whom the** LORD **calls**.*

In Acts 2:17 Joel's "and it shall come to pass *afterward*" becomes "And in the *last days* it shall be." The death, burial, resurrection, and ascension of Jesus to the right hand of God, accompanied by the outpouring of the Holy Spirit on Pentecost, was the *beginning* of *the end*, the "Eschaton," or "last day(s)." Whereas from an Old Testament perspective the "latter times" looked like a series of events happening within a short period of time, from a New Testament perspective we understand that the "latter days" will continue until Messiah comes *a second time*. This extended period of eschatological fulfillment can help explain the sequence of events we see in prophets like Joel, Zechariah, and Ezekiel.

Omitted by Peter, Joel 2:32 associates the salvation being described in 2:28-32 with "Mount Zion" and "Jerusalem." It is a common understanding of New Testament inaugurated eschatology that many of the promised blessings found in the Old Testament have only been fulfilled *in part* and will not come to pass *fully* until Jesus returns. But the partial fulfillment of such promises means that their fulfillment has *already begun*. Thus, there is a sense in which the promised blessings can be said to be "now" even if their complete fulfillment is "not yet."

For example, a common theme of Old Testament prophecy was the expectation of dwelling "securely" in Zion, e.g., Jer 23:6, 32:37, 33:16, et al. This security would be assured by the presence of the LORD in Zion, the holy city. In Christ, the saved are provided a similar kind of security through the presence of the indwelling of the Holy Spirit:

Eph 1:13-14
> ¹³*In him you also, when you heard the word of truth, the gospel of your salvation, and believed in him,* **were sealed with the promised Holy Spirit,** ¹⁴**who is the guarantee of our inheritance until we acquire possession of it,** *to the praise of his glory.*

Rom 8:12-13
> ¹²*So then, brothers, we are debtors, not to the flesh, to live according to the flesh.* ¹³*For if you live according to the flesh you will die, but* **if by the Spirit you put to death the deeds of the body, you will live.**

1 Cor 10:13b
> ¹³ᵇ **God is faithful, and he will not let you be tempted** *beyond your ability, but with the temptation he* **will also provide the way of escape,** *that you may be able to endure it.*

Not only is the presence of the indwelling of the Holy Spirit a source of security for the believer, it is a means by which God presently dwells *in the midst* of His people, making His people in Christ a *spiritual* temple:

1 John 3:24

> ²⁴Whoever keeps his commandments abides in God, and God in him. And by this we know that **he abides in us, by the Spirit whom he has given us.**

2 Cor 6:16b

> ¹⁶ᵇFor **we are the temple of the living God;** as God said,
> > "I will make my dwelling among them
> > and walk among them,
> > and I will be their God,
> > and they shall be my people.

Eph 2:22

> ²²In him you also are **being built together into a dwelling place for God by the Spirit.**

In Christ, God's people have *already* begun to experience the salvation that was the eschatological hope of Israel:

2 Cor 6:1-2

> ¹Working together with him, then, we appeal to you not to receive the grace of God in vain. ²For he says,
> > "In a favorable time I listened to you,
> > and in a day of salvation I have helped you."
> Behold, **now is the favorable time;** behold,
> > **now is the day of salvation.**

1 Pet 1:8-12

> ⁸Though you have not seen him, you love him. Though you do not now see him, you believe in him and rejoice with joy that is inexpressible and filled with glory, ⁹obtaining the outcome of your faith, **the salvation of your souls.**
> ¹⁰Concerning this salvation, the prophets who prophesied about the grace that was to be yours searched

> and inquired carefully, ¹¹inquiring what person or time the Spirit of Christ in them was indicating when he predicted **the sufferings of Christ and the subsequent glories.** ¹²it was revealed to them that **they were serving not themselves but you, in the things that have now been announced to you through those who preached the good news to you by the Holy Spirit sent from heaven,** things into which angels long to look.

Tit 2:11-13
> ¹¹For the grace of God has appeared, **bringing salvation for all people,** ¹²training us to renounce ungodliness and worldly passions, and to live self-controlled, upright, and godly lives **in the present age,** ¹³**waiting for** our blessed hope, **the appearing of the glory of our great God and Savior Jesus Christ,**

In various ways the New Testament Church has *already* begun to experience many of the blessings promised by God's prophets long ago. In 2 Cor 6:2 Paul says the day of salvation, quoting Isa 49:8, is *"Now."* Peter, too, referring to the salvation that was prophesied long ago, says that it has "*now* been announced…through those who preached the good news." But Paul tells Titus that while salvation has "appeared" we are still "waiting for…the appearing of the glory of…Jesus Christ." So, the promised salvation is both "now" and "not yet."

And because it is still in part "not yet" we find ourselves facing trials and tribulations, still being subjected to hostile powers, what Paul calls "the cosmic powers over this present darkness, …the spiritual forces of evil in the heavenly places," Eph 6:12. In Jesus' eschatological discourse in Matthew 24 he told the disciples that when they saw the destruction of Jerusalem that "the end is not yet," meaning that they should not take it as a sign of the Lord's second coming, v. 7. Instead, the turmoil associated with the destruction of Jerusalem was simply "the beginning of the birth pains," v. 8. Then, in vv. 9-14 Jesus describes an indeterminant time period during which God's people will be subjected to tribulation and persecution:

> [9]*"Then **they will deliver you up to tribulation and put you to death**, and **you will be hated by all nations** for my name's sake.* [10]*And then **many will fall away** and betray one another and hate one another.* [11]*And many false prophets will arise and lead many astray.* [12]*And because **lawlessness will be increased**, the love of many will grow cold.* [13]***But the one who endures to the end will be saved**.* [14]*And this gospel of the kingdom will be proclaimed throughout the whole world **as a testimony to all nations, and then the end will come**.*

This indeterminate period is what the New Testament calls "the last days," Acts 2:17, cf. 2 Tim 3:1, Heb 1:2, 1 Pet 1:5, 20, 2 Pet 3:3, Jude 18, 1 John 2:18. The "last days" which precede the *final* coming of the LORD in glory correspond to Old Testament texts which describe the returning exiles in Zion under attack by hostile nations. *We* are the returning exiles, who have "come to Mount Zion," Heb 12:22-24, and are facing the tribulation of hostile spiritual forces as we wait for the Lord's second coming, to consummate the establishment of God's Kingdom on earth.

This explanation for Old Testament texts describing the returning exiles in Zion under attack by hostile nations as being associated with the period of messianic "birth pains" fits well with the apocalyptic depiction of the end-times in the book of Revelation. Much of the main "apocalyptic" portion of the book, chapters 6-19, are visions depicting divine judgment and conflict during the "last days." God's people are under attack, and these visions are designed to encourage perseverance and provide assurance that the faithful will emerge victorious. Chapter 20 presents a view of all this that fits with viewing "the last days" as a time when the faithful are under attack, but can expect God to eventually vindicate the righteous and punish the wicked. Verses 4-6 describe a "millennial" kingdom where those who have been "redeemed from the earth," cf. Rev 14:3-5, are described as seated on thrones, reigning with Jesus as he rules the nations, cf. Rev 2:26-27, 3:21.[66] Those who have died and are now in Heaven ("the first resurrection") enjoy an enhanced measure of rest and security while they wait for God to bring to conclusion the ingathering of the exiles and the pilgrimage of the nations, Rev 6:17, 7:13-17, described more fully in Revelation chapters 21-22. The continuing tribulation on earth during this time corresponds to those Old Testament passages showing the returned exiles in Zion under attack.

---

[66] The subjects of 20:4-6 are described as "those who had been beheaded for the testimony of Jesus and for the word of God, and those who had not worshipped the beast or its image and had not received its mark on their foreheads or hands." Some try to limit this to a single group of *martyrs*, but the second clause (those not receiving the mark of the beast) is introduced with a demonstrative pronoun (the ESV's "and *those* who had not") which indicates that it is a second group, likely intended to represent all the rest of the redeemed who have died in a state of grace, Rev 14:13. The reading being offered above corresponds to the *amillennial* view of Rev 20:4-6, in contrast to either premillennialism or postmillennialism.

Verses 4-6 of Revelation 20 are followed with a final end-time destruction of the wicked, vv. 7-10, that is clearly intended to correspond in some way to Ezekiel 38-39:

> [7]*And when the thousand years are ended, Satan will be released from his prison* [8]*and will come out to deceive the nations that are at the four corners of the earth, Gog and Magog, to gather them for battle; their number is like the sand of the sea.* [9]*And they marched up over the broad plain of the earth and surrounded the camp of the saints and the beloved city, but fire came down from heaven and consumed them,* [10]*and the devil who had deceived them was thrown into the lake of fire and sulfur where the beast and the false prophet were, and they will be tormented day and night forever and ever.*

I think it is at least questionable, and perhaps even doubtful, that depictions like this are intended to be taken as literally predicting an end-time apocalyptic battle that will play out *in real time* on earth at the close of this age. A strong presumption against this is Jesus' teaching that the end will come quickly, like a thief in the night, catching the unprepared off guard. Relatedly, depictions of final judgment by Paul suggest an end that occurs not just unexpectedly, but quickly (as in 1 Thess 5:2-3, 2 Thess 1:7-8, 2:8).

A second consideration is that the *details* of the various depictions of an end-time apocalyptic battle disagree, suggesting that the depictions are *figurative,* intending only to assure believers that God will someday act decisively to judge the wicked, bring this age to a close, and usher in the world to come. Meanwhile, the image of an ingathering of God's people over a time period during which Satan leads hostile powers to afflict the redeemed fits well with the New Testament's depiction of an extended period of "birth pains" during which the gospel is preached to the whole world, and with Old Testament depictions of hostile forces arranged against the exiles who have returned to Zion. Any cognitive dissonance occasioned by the Old Testament depictions of exiles returning to Zion, only to be attacked by hostile forces, is resolved by the New Testament revelation of a now/not yet inauguration of the "last days."

ZION'S STORY

7 EPILOGUE

Zion's Story is about God wanting a *place* to dwell *in the midst* of His creation so that He might receive the praises of its glory. Several texts make this desire clear and explicit, including:

Ezek 43:7a, 9
> ⁷*and he said to me, "Son of man, this is the place of my throne and the place of the soles of my feet,* **where I will dwell in the midst of the people of Israel forever.**
> ⁹*Now let them put away their whoring and the dead bodies of their kings far from me,* **and I will dwell in their midst forever.**

Psa 132:13-14
> ¹³***For the L**ORD **has chosen Zion;***
>   *he has desired it for his* **dwelling place:**
> ¹⁴***"This is my resting place forever;***
>   *here I will dwell, for I have desired it."*

Throughout this study we have contended that "Zion" refers to a place on *earth*, not Heaven. Not the earth as we know it now, but a *new* earth, the new earth that we read about in Isa 65:17, 66:22, 2 Pet 3:13, and Rev 21:1. But this runs contrary to what most Christians believe about eternity. Most believe that the present earth will cease to be (i.e., "annihilated") at the Second Coming and that the redeemed will spend eternity in Heaven. From personal experience, I know how firm this belief is, and how hard it will be for many to accept what I am saying. But if you truly want to understand what scripture reveals about the matter, you need to *seriously* consider the possibility that what I am saying is what the word of God says.

In the preface I indicated I would describe various "hermeneutic keys" that lead me to believe that my reading of what scripture has to say about this matter is not just probable, but, to me, is beyond reasonable doubt. But before I do that, I want to encourage the reader to remember what was said about the Bereans in Acts 17:11:

> [11]*Now these Jews were more noble than those in Thessalonica; they received the word with all eagerness, examining the Scriptures daily* **to see if these things were so.**

Please note well what is said here. Paul was telling the Bereans (and those in the other cities where he took the gospel) what the scriptures were saying. And, if the reaction of the Jews in Thessalonica is any indication, what he was saying was *contrary* to how the Jews, *including the Bereans*, understood the scriptures. Now, what is the *typical* response when a believer is confronted with teaching that runs contrary to what they believe? I know from long personal experience that the typical response to being confronted with something contrary to what one believes is to search the scriptures for evidence that what is being said is *not so*. While one might believe that they are simply being sincere and earnest in "contending for the truth," searching the scriptures to show that something is *not so* is *dangerous* and is contrary to the "Berean spirit."

Searching the scriptures to show that something is *not so* is almost guaranteed to result in what is known as *confirmation bias*. Confirmation bias is the tendency to interpret evidence in a way that confirms one's prior beliefs about something. It has often been said, and not without a lot of truth to it, that if you search the scriptures long and hard enough, you can find evidence to support whatever you want the scriptures to support. A mind overtaken by confirmation bias will tend to discount any reading of scripture that conflicts with one's prior beliefs, and will read *into* scripture meaning and evidence for beliefs that are not there. If you think that this cannot happen to you, you are only fooling yourself. We have all done this, to one degree or another. I write from experience.

So, I ask you to follow the example of the Bereans: approach what I have been saying from the standpoint that it *is so*, i.e., that what I have been saying just *might* be a reasonable, and even compelling, understanding of scripture. Carefully consider the following "hermeneutic keys" that I will offer as a basis for why I think that our eternal destiny is not "in Heaven" but "in Zion," on a "new earth," as depicted in Rev 21:1-5a:

> [1]*Then **I saw a new heaven and a new earth**, for the first heaven and the first earth had passed away, and the sea was no more.* [2]*And **I saw the holy city, new Jerusalem, coming down out of heaven** from God, prepared as a bride adorned for her husband.* [3]*And I*

heard a loud voice from the throne saying, "Behold, the dwelling place of God is with man. He will dwell with them, and they will be his people, and God himself will be with them as their God. [4] *He will wipe away every tear from their eyes, and death shall be no more, neither shall there be mourning, nor crying, nor pain anymore, for the former things have passed away."* [5a] *And he who was seated on the throne said, "Behold, I am making all things new."*

As I work through these hermeneutic keys, I will address *briefly* common objections that people often have to the view presented here. I am confident enough in the power of these hermeneutic keys that objections can be dealt with easily and quickly.

Hermeneutic Key #1
The Old Testament doctrine of the eternity of creation

In my estimation, the most important hermeneutic key to a proper understanding of our eternal destiny is what the Old Testament teaches about the eternity of creation. We covered this in chapter 4 (pp. 46-55) and will not repeat here everything that was said there. I think the evidence presented there is at least reasonable, and even compelling. Here I will address the most common objection I hear when presenting this evidence, and offer a couple of further considerations.

Whenever I have had the opportunity to present what the Old Testament teaches about the eternity of creation, the most common response is: "What about 2 Peter 3?" One could ask: "Well, what about it?" To which the reply would likely be: "Well, 2 Pet 3:10-12 teaches that one day the earth, and the present cosmos, will be *completely* destroyed, as in annihilated." But, does it?

Before I answer that question, let me say this. *If* 2 Pet 3:10-12 teaches the annihilation of all creation except humanity, then we have an apparent *contradiction* between the Old Testament and the New Testament. The material presented in chapter 4 on the eternity of creation is compelling. Is a reading of annihilation in 2 Pet 3:10-12 equally compelling? One principle of biblical hermeneutics is that if two scriptures *appear* to contradict each other, then we are misreading one (or possibly both) of them. Is it *possible* that 2 Pet 3:10-12 is *not* teaching the annihilation of the cosmos? Yes, it is possible, and if we are to avoid setting scripture against itself, this is the way we should read 2 Pet 3:10-12.

I said I would *briefly* address objections like this. I could easily write an entire chapter (or two) on this matter, discussing at length why reading annihilation into 2 Pet 3:10-12 is unwarranted. But briefly, my argument would be that none of the verbs that describe the "destruction" under consideration in 2 Peter 3 *necessarily* imply annihilation. The translation of 2 Pet 3:10-12 is notoriously complicated, and I am not entirely happy with any common version, but the main points I would make here can be made with the following versions (NABRE and NASB):[67]

---

[67] My concern with the ESV here is two-fold:

> [10]But the day of the Lord will come like a thief, and then the heavens will pass away with a roar, and the **heavenly bodies** will **be burned up** and dissolved, and the earth and the works that are done on it **will be exposed**. [11]Since all these things are thus to be dissolved, what sort of people ought you to be in lives of holiness and godliness, [12]waiting for and hastening the coming of the day

¹⁰*But the day of the Lord will come like a thief, and then the heavens will **pass away** with a mighty roar and the **elements** will be **dissolved** by **fire**, and the earth and everything done on it will be **found out**. ¹¹Since everything is to be **dissolved** in this way, what sort of persons ought [you] to be, conducting yourselves in holiness and devotion, ¹²waiting for and hastening the coming of the day of God, because of which the heavens will be **dissolved** in flames and the elements melted by fire.* [NABRE]

¹⁰*But the day of the Lord will come like a thief, in which the heavens will **pass away** with a roar and the **elements** will be **destroyed** with **intense heat**, and the earth and its works will be **discovered**. ¹¹Since all these things are to be **destroyed** in this way, what sort of people ought you to be in holy conduct and*

---

of God, because of which the heavens will be set on fire and dissolved, and **the heavenly bodies** will melt as they burn!

The ESV translates the Greek word *stoicheia* [Strong's #G4747] in vv. 10 and 12 as "heavenly bodies." This is more a case of *interpretation* than *translation*. The standard *translation* of *stoicheia* is "elements," as reflected in the KSV, ASV, NABRE, NIV, and many other translations. After a thorough discussion of the various usages of *stoicheia*, TDNT, 7:686, concludes: "In 2 Pet. 3:10, 12, the only possible meaning is 'elements' or 'stars'" (citations omitted), but goes on only to mention the case for "elements." Previously TDNT, 7:681, acknowledged a meaning for *stoicheia* as "stars" or "constellations," but only in late antiquity, e.g., after the time of the New Testament.

My second concern is the translation of *kausoumena* [Strong's #G2741] in v. 10 as "be burned up." This is not a case of interpretation, but of *mistranslation*. The word *kausoumena* is a participle, a verb functioning as an adverb or adjective. Its action *describes* the verb translated as "dissolve," and does not constitute separate and distinct action as the ESV renders it. Thus, the elements are being "dissolved with fervent heat" or "dissolved with fire." They are not being "burned up," but "dissolved" (by heat or fire).

> godliness, ¹²*looking for and hastening the coming of the day of God, because of which the heavens will be **destroyed** by **burning**, and the elements will **melt** with **intense heat**!*

There is nothing in the expression "pass away" (v. 10) that necessarily implies annihilation.⁶⁸ Nor does the Greek word translated "dissolved" (NABRE) or "destroyed" (NASB) necessarily imply annihilation. If I tell you my house was "destroyed" by a fire, and you drive by it to inspect the damage, you will not be expecting to see nothing at all (as if it had completely ceased to be), but a smoldering pile of rubble. The NABRE's translation "dissolved" is technically a better translation than the NASB here because the kind of destruction implied by the underlying Greek word is that of untying or loosening what binds something together, e.g., dissolution or dissolving.⁶⁹ That is not annihilation. The other main verb of action in v. 12 is that of "melting," a type of "destruction"

---

⁶⁸ The same Greek word, *parerchomai* [Strong's #G3928], is used in Jms 1:10 to describe human mortality: "because like a flower of the grass he [a rich man] will pass away." Few Christians would insist that when humans "pass away" that they are annihilated.

⁶⁹ In its most basic or literal sense the Greek *lyō* [Strong's #G3089] means to "loose, untie bonds," BDAG 606, 1. Further lexical insight as to its use in 2 Pet 3:10-12:

> "to reduce something by violence into its components,... Of the parts of the universe as it is broken up and destroyed in the final conflagration, 2 Pet 3:10-12." BDAG 607, 3.
>
> "to loosen, undo, dissolve, anything bound, tied, or compacted together...to dissolve something coherent into parts, to destroy [citing all three occurrences in 2 Pet 3:10-12.," Thayer, 385, 3.
>
> "to destroy or reduce something to ruin by tearing down or breaking into pieces – 'to destroy, to tear down, to break to pieces.'" LN, 2:234, 20:53.

that involves a change of state, not annihilation. The two types of action, dissolution and melting, are being *caused* by fire (cf. 2 Pet 3:7), but nothing is being said that necessarily implies annihilation.

Since nothing in 2 Pet 3:10-12 *necessitates* reading the text to imply annihilation, there is no good reason not to read the Old Testament texts that imply the eternity of creation to *mean exactly what they say*. When God created the heavens and the earth in Gen 1:1, 2:1, He "established" His creation so that it would "stand firm" forever and ever. Yes, in both the Old Testament and New Testament we have scripture teaching that God will bring judgment upon the earth that is cosmic and cataclysmic in nature. But as we saw in chapter 4, Psa 75:3 and 104:5 (just to mention those two), affirm that God will not let such judgment *totally* destroy or annihilate His creation.

To those who think God is planning to annihilate His creation, I ask you this: why would He do that? Few things in scripture are more closely associated with God's glory and majesty than His creation. He is, above all else, a "Creator God," a "God who Creates," Rev 4:11, Neh 9:6, Psa 33:6, Isa 42:5, 44:24, 45:8, 12, 18. Imagine an artist or sculptor who has created something so well known that it comes to be identified as their greatest work. Would they completely destroy their greatest work?

God created the heavens and the earth that He might receive the praises of its glory. *Repeatedly*, scripture tells us of creation *praising* God:

"The heavens declare the glory of God, and the sky

None of this implies annihilation.

above proclaims his handiwork," **Psa 19:1**. "All the earth worships you and sings praises to you; they sing praises to your name," **Psa 66:4**. "O LORD, how manifold are your works! In wisdom have you made them all; the earth is full of your creatures. Here is the sea, great and wide, which teems with creatures innumerable, living things both small and great." **Psa 104:24-25**. "Let the heavens be glad, and let the earth rejoice; let the sea roar, and all that fills it; let the field exult, and everything in it! Then shall all the trees of the forest sing for joy," **Psa 96:11-12**. "Let heaven and earth praise him, the seas and everything that moves in them," **Psa 69:34**. "The LORD reigns, let the earth rejoice; let the many coastlands be glad! ... The heavens proclaim his righteousness, and all the peoples see his glory," **Psa 97:1, 6**. "The wild beasts will honor me, the jackals and the ostriches, for I give water in the wilderness, rivers in the desert, to give drink to my chosen people, the people whom I formed for myself that they might declare my praise," **Isa 43:20-21**.

"Let the heavens praise your wonders, O LORD, your faithfulness in the assembly of the holy ones," **Psa 89:5**. "And I heard every creature in heaven and on earth and under the earth and in the sea, and all that is in them, saying, 'To him who sits on the throne and to the Lamb be blessing and honor and glory and might forever and ever!'," **Rev 5:13**. And the most famous paean of them all: "Praise the LORD! Praise the LORD from the heavens; praise him in the heights! Praise him, all his angels; praise him, all his hosts! Praise him, sun and moon, praise him, all you shining stars! Praise him, you highest heavens, and you waters above the heavens! Let them praise the name of the LORD! ... Praise the LORD from the earth, you great

> *sea creatures and all deeps, fire and hail, snow and mist, stormy wind fulfilling his word! Mountains and all hills, fruit trees and all cedars! Beasts and all livestock, creeping things and flying birds! Kings of the earth and all peoples, princes and all rulers of the earth! Young men and maidens together, old men and children! Let them praise the name of the* LORD, *for his name alone is exalted; his majesty is above earth and heaven,"* **Psa 148:1-5a, 7-13**.

What kind of God would design such a wondrous creation, call it "very good," Gen 1:28, only to someday destroy it all as if never existed, and mattered even less? Not the LORD God of the Bible!

Our "hope" and the "glory" that is to be revealed to us in eternity is very much tied to the destiny of creation:

Rom 5:1-5
> [1]*Therefore, since we have been justified by faith, we have peace with God through our Lord Jesus Christ.* [2]*Through him we have also obtained access by faith into this grace in which we stand,* **and we rejoice in hope of the glory of God.**[70] [3]*Not only that, but we rejoice in our sufferings, knowing that suffering produces endurance,* [4]*and endurance produces character, and character produces* **hope,** [5]*and* **hope** *does not put us to shame, because God's love has been poured into our hearts through the Holy Spirit who has been given to us.*

Rom 8:18-25
> [18]*For I consider that the sufferings of this present time are not worth comparing* **with the glory that is**

---
[70] Cf. Rev 21:11, 23.

> to be revealed to us. **¹⁹For the creation waits with eager longing** for the revealing of the sons of God. **²⁰For the creation was subjected to futility,** not willingly, but because of him who subjected it, in **hope ²¹that the creation itself will be set free from its bondage to corruption and obtain the freedom of the glory of the children of God.** **²²**For we know that **the whole creation has been groaning together in the pains of childbirth until now.** ²³And not only the creation, but we ourselves, who have the firstfruits of the Spirit, groan inwardly as we wait eagerly for adoption as sons, the redemption of our bodies. ²⁴For in this **hope** we were saved. Now hope that is seen is not hope. For who hopes for what he sees? ²⁵But if **we hope for what we do not see,** we await for it with patience.

Why would creation be waiting "with eager longing" for eternity if its fate in eternity is to be annihilated?

Given all of this I find it hard to imagine an eternity in which most of God's wonderful creation has been annihilated and no longer exists. The Old Testament doctrine of the eternity of creation is not just the most reasonable way to understand what we considered on this score in chapter 4, I think it is the only way to make any sense of the matter. Once we recognize and understand the power of this hermeneutic key, the rest of Zion's story quickly falls into place.

Hermeneutic Key #2
The LORD's Promise to Abraham

I am combining under this heading three separate Old Testament themes that we have covered in this study:

1) The reunification of Judah and Israel.
2) The return of the exiles and the pilgrimage of the

nations.

3) The "land promise."

In chapter 2 we only looked at a couple of texts about the reunification of Judah and Israel (Jer 3:18, Ezek 37:15-28, along with Paul and Peter's use of Hos 1:10 and 2:23, see pp. 17-19 above). But the theme is ubiquitous, as a few more examples will show:

Isa 11:12
> [12] He will raise a signal for the nations
> and **will assemble the banished of Israel,**
> **and gather the dispersed of Judah**

Hos 1:11
> [11] And **the children of Judah and the children of Israel shall be gathered together,** and they shall appoint for themselves one head. And they shall go up from the land, for great shall be the day of Jezreel.

Oba 1:20-21
> [20] **The exiles** of this host of **the people of Israel** shall
> **possess the land** of the Canaanites as far as Zarephath,
> and **the exiles of Jerusalem** who are in Sepharad
> shall possess the cities of the Negeb.
> [21] Saviors shall go up to Mount Zion
> to rule Mount Esau,
> and **the kingdom** shall be the LORD's.

Zech 10:6
> [6] "I will strengthen **the house of Judah,**
> and I will save **the house of Joseph.**
> **I will bring them back** because I have
> compassion on them,
> and they shall be as though I had not rejected them,
> for I am the LORD their God and I will answer them.

Mic 2:12

> ¹²*I will **surely assemble all of you, O Jacob;***
> ***I will gather the remnant of Israel;***
> *I will set them **together***
> *like sheep in a fold,*
> *like a flock in its pasture,*
> *a noisy multitude of men.*

Amos 9:11, 14-15
> ¹¹*"In that day I will raise up*
> ***the booth of David** that is fallen*
> *and repair its breaches,*
> *and raise up its ruins*
> *and **rebuild it as in the days of old,***
> ¹⁴*I will restore the fortunes of **my people Israel,***
> *and they shall rebuild the ruined cities and inhabit them; they shall plant vineyards and drink their wine, and they shall make gardens and eat their fruit.*
> ¹⁵*I will plant them on their land,*
> *and they shall never again be uprooted*
> *out of the land that I have given them,"*
> *says the* LORD *your God.*

Others could be noted. And in many of them, a return to "the land" is prominent, such as:

Ezek 36:24, 28, 33-36
> ²⁴*I will take you from the nations and gather you from all the countries and **bring you into your own land.***
>
> ²⁸***You shall dwell in the land that I gave to your fathers,** and you shall be my people, and I will be your God.*
>
> ³³*"Thus says the Lord* GOD: *On the day that I cleanse you from all your iniquities, I will cause the cities to be inhabited, and the waste places shall be rebuilt.*
> ³⁴ *And **the land** that was desolate shall be tilled, instead of being the desolation that it was in the sight*

of all who passed by. ³⁵And they will say, **'This land that was desolate has become like the garden of Eden,** and the waste and desolate and ruined cities are now fortified and inhabited.' ³⁶Then the nations that are left all around you shall know that I am the LORD; I have rebuilt the ruined places and replanted that which was desolate. I am the LORD; I have spoken, and I will do it."

Ezek 37:20-22, 25-26

²⁰When the sticks on which you write are in your hand before their eyes, ²¹then say to them, Thus says the Lord GOD: Behold, I will take the people of Israel from the nations among which they have gone, and will gather them from all around, and **bring them to their own land**. ²²And I will make them one **nation in the land**, on the mountains of Israel. And one king shall be king over them all, and they shall be no longer two nations, and no longer divided into two kingdoms.

²⁵They shall **dwell in the land** that I gave to my servant Jacob, where your fathers lived. They and their children and their children's children shall dwell there forever, and David my servant shall be their prince forever. ²⁶I will make a covenant of peace with them. It shall be an everlasting covenant with them. And **I will set them in their land** and multiply them, and will set my sanctuary in their midst forevermore.

This is important because it indicates there is a "land promise" that remains yet to be fulfilled. The reunion of Judah and Israel and the return of the exiles to the land are prophetic of aspects to God's promise to Abraham that are being fulfilled in Christ.

The "land promise" has often been dismissed as relevant to our faith and hope with the claim that it was completely fulfilled in the conquest of Canaan during the time of Joshua. This claim is based on a misreading and misunderstanding of two passages in the book of Joshua:

Josh 21:43-45
> [43]**Thus the LORD gave to Israel all the land that he swore to give to their fathers.** And they took possession of it, and they settled there. [44]And the LORD gave them rest on every side just **as he had sworn to their fathers.** Not one of all their enemies had withstood them, for the LORD had given all their enemies into their hands. [45]**Not one word of all the good promises that the LORD had made to the house of Israel had failed;** all came to pass.

Josh 23:14
> [14] "And now I am about to go the way of all the earth, and you know in your hearts and souls, all of you, that **not one word has failed of all the good things that the LORD your God promised concerning you.** All have come to pass for you; not one of them has failed.

The "fathers" here, and the promises the LORD to "made to the house of Israel" (21:45) do not refer to the "Patriarchs" (Abraham, Isaac, and Jacob), but to their "fathers" from *the time of Moses*, Josh 11:23:

> [23]So Joshua took the whole land, according to all that **the LORD had spoken to Moses.** And Joshua gave it for an inheritance to Israel according to their tribal allotments. And the land had rest from war.

Yahweh promised through Moses in the final words of the "Book of the Covenant" (Exodus 20-23, specifically 23:20-

33) that He would drive out the nations in Canaan. Anticipating this victorious conquest of Canaan, the LORD spoke to Moses in Num 34:2-12 as to the borders of the land that they would conquer. It is *these* promises, *to Israel* through *Moses* that Josh 21:43-45 and 23:14 claim were fulfilled, not the *original* "land promise" to Abraham, Isaac, and Jacob.

At best, the conquest of Canaan under Joshua was a *type* of the fulfillment of the land promise to the Patriarchs, the *antitype* being fulfilled *in Christ*. Of the promise made to Abraham, Gen 18:17-19 says:

> [17]The LORD said, "Shall I hide from Abraham what I am about to do, [18]seeing that Abraham shall surely become a great and mighty nation, and all the nations of the earth shall be blessed in him? [19]For I have chosen him, **that he may command his children and his household after him to keep the way of the LORD by doing righteousness and justice, so that the LORD may bring to Abraham what he has promised him.**"

God's promise to Abraham is here conditioned on his "children and his household after him to keep the way of the LORD by doing righteousness and justice." As a nation, Israel never satisfied this condition, *otherwise* there would have been no need for Christ. As Paul said in 2 Cor 1:19-20:

> [19]For the Son of God, Jesus Christ, whom we proclaimed among you, Silvanus and Timothy and I, was not Yes and No, but in him it is always Yes. [20]**For all the promises of God find their Yes in him.** That is why it is through him that we utter our Amen to God for his glory.

All the promises of God, including all aspects of God's promise to Abraham, find their "Yes" in Christ.

Therefore, a "land promise" remains for *us* who have set our hope on Christ. The repeated references to "land" in the Old Testament prophecies regarding the reunification of Judah and Israel and the return of the exiles (to Zion) apply to *our* hope for eternity. The "land" that these prophecies allude to has nothing to do with Heaven, but with a *place* on earth where God will dwell in the midst of His people, i.e., Zion, God's holy hill, Jerusalem. It is the land where Ezek 37:26b will finally be fulfilled:

> *And I will set them **in their land** and multiply them,*
> *and will set my sanctuary **in their midst** forevermore.*

Which brings us to our next hermeneutic key. But to recap this one, the numerous Old Testament prophecies that promise a reunion of Judah and Israel and a return of the exiles to the land have their fulfillment *in Christ* (and not in the return from Babylonian captivity)[71]. Thus, they speak to *us* today, and to our faith and hope for tomorrow, and eternity. They warrant our serious study and reflection. And if we do that, we will see a much different picture of the glory God has prepared for us than simply spending eternity in Heaven.

Hermeneutic Key #3
The Locational Significance of "In the Midst of"

Throughout this study, but especially in chapter 2, we have seen repeated emphasis upon God's desire to dwell

---

[71] Cf. previous remarks on pp. 39-40 and footnote 53.

in the midst of His people. This is a significant hermeneutic key for what it implies about the location or direction of movement in God and humanity coming together forever in the age to come. In the final paragraph of the previous hermeneutic key we referred to Ezek 37:26b, now repeated with more of the context in which it occurs, vv. 24-28:

> ²⁴*"My servant David shall be king over them, and they shall all have one shepherd. They shall walk in my rules and be careful to obey my statutes. ²⁵They shall dwell **in the land** that I gave to my servant Jacob, where your fathers lived. They and their children and their children's children shall dwell there forever, and David my servant shall be their prince forever. ²⁶I will make a covenant of peace with them. It shall be an everlasting covenant with them. And **I will set them in their land** and multiply them, and **will set my sanctuary in their midst forevermore**. ²⁷My dwelling place shall be with them, and I will be their God, and they shall be my people. ²⁸Then the nations will know that I am the* LORD *who sanctifies Israel, **when my sanctuary is in their midst forevermore**."*

We have examined this passage before (pp. 19-20) but it is such an important passage for understanding our eschatological hope and future that it warrants full consideration again. This time, note well what is said in vv. 26 and 28 about *where* the LORD will set His sanctuary: "in *their* midst." Not "in *His* midst," but "in *their* midst." The same description of where God will set His sanctuary is found in Ezek 43:7a, 9:[72]

---

[72] We have now alluded to this text over a dozen times (and will yet again below), indicative of its significance. A complete listing of

> *⁷ᵃand he said to me, "Son of man, this is **the place of my throne and the place of the soles of my feet**, where I will dwell in the midst of the people of Israel forever.*
>
> *⁹Now let them put away their whoring and the dead bodies of their kings far from me, and **I will dwell in their midst forever.***

While Heaven is referred to as a sanctuary in scripture, it has existed since the beginning of creation and is not something that moves about. So, when Ezekiel 37, vv. 26 and 28, speak of God setting His sanctuary somewhere, it is not a reference to Heaven; it is a reference to God setting His sanctuary in the midst of His people, in *their* midst. This is the LORD being with His people where *they* are. And what is especially important about this is this is precisely the image depicted for us in the final consummation of our faith and hope in Rev 21:1-3:

> *¹Then I saw a new heaven and a new earth, for the first heaven and the first earth had passed away, and the sea was no more. ²**And I saw the holy city, new Jerusalem, coming down out of heaven from God**, prepared as a bride adorned for her husband. ³And I heard a loud voice from the throne saying, "Behold, **the dwelling place of God is with man. He will dwell with them**, and they will be his people, and **God himself will be with them as their God**.*

Verse 3 explicitly depicts God "with man," and dwelling "with them," not man going to Heaven to be "with God" and dwelling "with God." And if that were not clear enough, this scene is not taking place in Heaven, but rather describes God and the new Jerusalem "coming down

---

pages where it appears can be found in the Scripture Index, p. 131.

out of heaven *from* God." It would be difficult to make what is being said here any plainer.

When the LORD sets His sanctuary in the midst of His creation and in the midst of His people, He will dwell with them in their natural, *intended*, habitat, *earth*:

Isa 45:18
> ¹⁸*For thus says the LORD,*
>   *who created the heavens*
> *(he is God!),*
>   **who formed the earth and made it**
> *(he established it;*
>   **he did not create it empty,**
>   **he formed it to be inhabited!**):
>   *"I am the LORD, and there is no other.*

Psa 115:16
> ¹⁶*The heavens are the LORD's heavens,*
>   *but* **the earth he has given to the children of man.**

The reference to God's purpose in creating the earth In Isa 45:18 "to be inhabited" is significant in light of Heb 2:5:

> ⁵*For it was not to angels that God* **subjected the world to come***, of which we are speaking.*

The Greek word translated as "world" in this verse is not the word most often translated "world" in the New Testament (*cosmos*). Here the Greek is *oikoumenē*, a word that in New Testament times was understood to refer to *the inhabited earth*.[73] The use of this word by the writer of Hebrews is a strong witness to the Old Testament understanding of the age to come as being *on earth*.

---

[73] See BDAG, 699-700, 1, 4; NIDNTTE, 3:476-478, Thayer, 441-42; Mounce's, 808-09; LN, 2:10, 1.39. Strong's #G3625.

God's own commentary about what is being depicted in Rev 21:1-3 follows in v. 5a:

> ⁵ᵃ*And he who was seated on the throne said, "Behold, **I am making all things new**."*

In context this can only refer to the new heaven and new earth of Rev 21:1. It would make no sense at all in reference to Heaven.

What is said about God dwelling in the midst of His people and His creation, and especially about dwelling "in *their* midst" is a powerful and important hermeneutic key in making sense of what scripture reveals about our faith and hope for eternity.

Hermeneutic Key #4
The Place of God's Throne and the Soles of His Feet

Another hermeneutic key that leads to the conclusion that our eternal destiny is on a renewed earth, rather than in Heaven, is the depiction of God's throne *on earth* and what is said about "the soles of his feet:"

Ezek 43:7a

> ⁷ᵃ*and he said to me, "Son of man, this is **the place of my throne and the place of the soles of my feet**, where I will dwell in the midst of the people of Israel forever.*

Jer 3:17

> ¹⁷***At that time Jerusalem shall be called the throne of the Lord**, and all nations shall gather to it, to the presence of the Lord in Jerusalem, and they shall no more stubbornly follow their own evil heart.*

Isa 60:13

> ¹³*The glory of Lebanon shall come to you,*
>   *the cypress, the plane, and the pine,*

*to beautify the place of my sanctuary,
and I will make the place of my feet glorious.*

The correlation of the throne of Ezek 43:7a and the Jerusalem of Jer 3:17 with the throne in the new Jerusalem of Rev 22:1-3 should be obvious. In chapter 2 (pp. 13-15) we discussed how unique is this depiction of the throne of God *on earth*. And that the *place* of God's throne being depicted here is *on earth* is made certain by the figure of it being *the place* of "the soles of [His] feet" (also discussed in chapter 2, p. 15).[74]

---

[74] Some readers of Zion's Story in draft raised concerns about how to justify appealing to a literal application of scripture in some cases (as here), with a spiritual application in others (such as treating the Old Testament prediction of a reunion of Israel and Judah as referring to the spiritual union of Jew and Gentile in Christ rather than a future literal restoration of Israel and Judah (as in premillennialism). If I can make a spiritual application of the latter, what is to stop others from making a spiritual application of a future "land" to eternity with God in Heaven? The decision of when to interpret something as "literal" and when to interpret it as "figurative" is not arbitrary. The choices I have made have been driven by *scripture*; they were not arbitrary. It is Paul, writing in Rom 9:25-26, and Peter, writing in 1 Pet 2:10, that compel me to a spiritual interpretation of Old Testament passages regarding the reunion of Israel and Judah. As for my belief that Zion as the eternal home of the redeemed is on a literal (but "new") earth, it is texts like Ezek 43:7, 9 and Isa 60:13, along with the evidence for the eternity of creation (cf. Hermeneutic Key #1), which compel me to conclude that our eternal home will be on a "literal" future earth, not in Heaven.

I put "literal" in quotes in the preceding sentence, because the real distinction is over whether our future home will be purely "spiritual" or whether it will also be "material" (but incorruptible). That which is "material" can be "spiritual" (to contend otherwise is Platonic dualism); e.g., the human institution of marriage is both "spiritual" and "physical," Heb 13:4, cf. Eph 5:25-33. A future Zion on a "new earth" (comprised of an incorruptible materiality) will be

Hermeneutic Key #5
Renewal, and the Restoration of Fortunes

A final hermeneutic key to understanding the nature of our eternal destiny and home we will consider is found in the concepts of renewal and the restoration of fortunes. In defense of the widespread belief that the Christian destiny is an eternity in Heaven, and in opposition to the view that "new heaven and new earth" means exactly what it says, some contend that the concept of "renewal" is never applied to the material cosmos in scripture, but only applied to humans, as in passages like Rom 12:2, Titus 3:5, 2 Cor 4:16, Eph 4:23, Col 3:10. They give no consideration to what is taught in scripture about the *cosmic* scope of God's work of redemption in Christ in passages like:

Rev 21:5a
> [5]*And he who was seated on the throne said, "Behold, **I am making all things new**."*

Eph 1:10
> [10]*as a plan for the fullness of time, to unite **all things** in him, **things in heaven and things on earth**.*

Col 1:16, 20
> [16]*For by him **all things were created, in heaven and on earth, visible and invisible**, whether thrones or dominions or rulers or authorities—all things were created through him and for him.*
>
> [20]*and through him to reconcile to himself **all things**,*

"spiritual" because the LORD will be in its midst, and it will be characterized by righteousness, 2 Pet 3:13. It is a false dichotomy to set "spiritual" and "material" against each other and insist that to be "spiritual" our eternal home can only be in Heaven.

> *whether on earth or in heaven, making peace by the blood of his cross.*

John 1:3
> ³*All things were made through him, and without him was not any thing made that was made.*

Acts 3:21
> ²¹*whom heaven must receive until the time for **restoring all the things about** which God spoke by the mouth of his holy prophets long ago.*

In the context of Rev 21:1-5, the "all things" that are being made "new" can be nothing other than the "new heaven and new earth" of v. 1. Those who defend the view that the Christian hope is an eternity in Heaven often dismiss the reference to "new heaven and new earth" as figurative language for Heaven. But in what world would *Heaven* have to be made "new?" Now, "heaven" is included in the "all things" of Eph 1:10 and Col 1:16, 20, but "heaven" in those passages should be understood to encompass the larger *spiritual* domain such as is indicated with the expression "heavenly places" in Ephesians (1:3, 20, 2:6, 3:10, 6:12) and *not* the specific "Heaven" where God is enthroned and where most Christians think they will spend eternity. That there has been rebellion in the larger spiritual domain that needs to be "reconciled" in Christ according to the "plan for the fulness of time" comes as no surprise. But no one can reasonably maintain that the Heaven where God is enthroned is part of what is being made "new" in Rev 21:1-5.

So, the attempt to dismiss the expression "new heaven and new earth" simply as a figure of speech for the Heaven from where God reigns over *all* creation (both spiritual and material) is without merit. That a specific word for "renew" is not used in Rev 21:5 is a baseless contention because "renewal" is *implicit* in the Greek word translated "making" in Rev 21:5. The word in question, *poieō*, is used in Rev 21:5 with the sense of making something *from* something, i.e., *reusing* existing material to make something "new."[75] Moreover, the "all things" of Rev 21:5 can only be understood in the sense of *all creation*. This is made clear by Col 1:16, 20 where "all things" embodies "all things created...in heaven and on earth, visible and invisible." God's "plan for the fulness of time" (Eph 1:3) is *cosmic* in scope, and encompasses *everything* that was "made" *in the beginning*, John 1:3.[76]

"Renewal" is also implicit in Peter's reference to "*restoring* all the things about which God spoke by the mouth of his holy prophets long ago," Acts 3:21. Peter may have in mind Old Testament texts that use a pair of Hebrew words that have been called a "restoration formula," idiomatically "to restore the fortunes of" or "bring about a restoration."[77] Examples of such texts include:

---

[75] So say the lexicons: BDAG, 839-40, 2.h.β; Thayer, 525, 2.a; cf. LN, 2: 514, 42.29, Strong's #G4160.

[76] The word translated "made" in the ESV of John 1:3 is different than the word translated "making" in Rev 21:5. In John 1:3 the relevant Greek word is *egeneto* [Strong's #G1096], better translated as "came/come *into being*" (CEB, LEB, NASB, NRSV, and others) or "created" (Mounce, NET Bible, CSB). Thus "all things" has reference to *everything* that was created *ex nihilo* ("out of/from nothing") in Gen 1:1, 2:1. In Rev 21:1-5 what was *originally* ("in the beginning") created from nothing is now being made *ex vetere* ("from the old"), e.g., *renewed*.

[77] The Hebrew words are *šûḇ* and *šᵉḇût*, Strong's #H7725 and #H7622. See NIDOTTE, 4: 58, 9.

Deut 30:3

³then the Lord your God will **restore your fortunes** and have mercy on you, and he will **gather you again** from all the peoples where the Lord your God has scattered you.

Psa 53:6

⁶Oh, that salvation for Israel would come out of **Zion**! When God **restores the fortunes** of his people, let **Jacob** rejoice, let **Israel** be glad.

Jer 29:14

¹⁴I will be found by you, declares the Lord, and I will **restore your fortunes** and **gather you from all the nations** and all the places where I have driven you, declares the Lord, and I will **bring you back to the place** from which I sent you into exile.

Jer 30:3

³For behold, **days are coming**, declares the Lord, when I will **restore the fortunes** of my people, **Israel** and **Judah**, says the Lord, and I will **bring them back to the land** that I gave to their fathers, and they shall take possession of it."

Jer 31:23

²³Thus says the Lord of hosts, the God of **Israel**: "Once more they shall use these words in **the land of Judah** and in its cities, when I **restore their fortunes**.

Ezek 39:25, 29

²⁵"Therefore thus says the Lord God: Now I will **restore the fortunes** of **Jacob** and have mercy on the whole house of **Israel**, and I will be jealous for my holy name... ²⁹And I will not hide my face anymore from them, when I pour out my Spirit upon the house of Israel, declares the Lord God."

Hos 6:11
> ¹¹*For you also, O Judah, a harvest is appointed.*
>   *When I **restore the fortunes** of my people,*

Joel 3:1
> ¹*"For behold, **in those days** and at that time, when I*
>   ***restore the fortunes of Judah and Jerusalem**,*

We have seen some of these passages before. Notice the overlap with other themes that we have been exploring, like the return of the exiles, from both Israel and Judah, to the land. Once again, because it is such an important point, these passages apply to *our* future, to *our* hope for eternity. We should not ignore what they are saying about it.

And what they are saying is that ultimate humanity's future is *all* about *restoring* humanity to the *glory* that Yahweh intended for it *in the beginning*. Nowhere is this more eloquently expressed than in Psalm 8:

> ¹*O LORD, our Lord,*
>   *how majestic is your name in all the earth!*
>   ***You have set your glory above the heavens.***
> ²*Out of the mouth of babies and infants,*
>   *you have established strength because of your*
>   *foes, to still the enemy and the avenger.*
> ³*When I look at your **heavens**, the work of your fingers,*
>   ***the moon and the stars, which you have***
>   ***set in place**,*
> ⁴*what is man that you are mindful of him,*
>   *and the son of man that you care for him?*
> ⁵*Yet you have made him a little lower*
>   *than the heavenly beings*
>   *and crowned him with glory and honor.*
> ⁶*You have given him dominion over the works of your*
>   *hands; you have put all things under his feet,*

> ⁷*all sheep and oxen,*
>   *and also the beasts of the field,*
> ⁸*the birds of the heavens, and the fish of the sea,*
>   *whatever passes along the paths of the seas.*
> ⁹*O LORD, our Lord,*
>   *how majestic is your name in all the earth!*

The LORD's *glory* is set "above the heavens." To humanity, though, He has given *the earth*, cf. Psa 115:16. In the beginning (Genesis 1) he "crowned" humanity "with glory and honor." Verses 6-8 of Psalm 8 recall the creation mandate of Gen 1:26-28. We know the rest of *that* story. Humanity sinned and fell from grace.

But God had "a plan for the fullness of time" that would *restore* humanity to the "glory and honor" that it had in the beginning, i.e., dominion over all of God's *creation*. That plan was to make "all things new" by reconciling "all things…in heaven and on earth, visible and invisible" through Christ. The writer of Hebrews describes this plan in language that envisages restoring humanity to the glory that it had in the beginning, through Christ, in Heb 2:5-10:

> ⁵*For it was not to angels that God subjected the world to come, of which we are speaking.* ⁶*It has been testified somewhere,*
>
>   *"What is man, that you are mindful of him,*
>   *or the son of man, that you care for him?*
> ⁷**You made him for a little while lower than the angels;**
>   **you have crowned him with glory and honor,**
> ⁸*putting everything in subjection under his feet."*
>
> *Now in putting everything in subjection to him, he left nothing outside his control. At present, we do not yet see everything in subjection to him.* ⁹ *But we see*

> him who for a little while was made lower than the angels, namely Jesus, crowned with glory and honor because of the suffering of death, so that by the grace of God he might taste death for everyone.
> ¹⁰For it was fitting that he, for whom and by whom all things exist, **in bringing many sons to glory**, should make the founder of their salvation perfect through suffering.

In "bringing many sons to glory" Jesus is *restoring* humanity to the *glory* it had *in the beginning*, a glory that put everything *on earth* "in subjection under his [humanity's] feet." To believe that someday God is going to destroy the earth such that it entirely ceases to be – i.e., is annihilated – is to *disbelieve* all that scripture is telling us about how God is *restoring* "all things" in Christ. To believe such a thing is to not understand Zion's story at all.

The Last Word

Zion's story is all about God creating a *place* to dwell in the midst of His creation *on earth*. It is about God fulfilling the *eternal purpose* for which the heavens and the earth were created *in the first place*. God knew humanity would fall from grace, and had a plan for the fullness of time that would undo all the wrong that was wrought in the world through sin and transgression. And what is so wonderful and marvelous about this plan is that the *latter glory* of God's creation would be even *greater* than its former glory. Think about what we see *now* when we behold the wonders of God's creation. The sun, moon, and stars, and with our modern technology billions of galaxies in the heavens above. The beauty of the earth with its seasons, land, sea, and sky teaming with *life* of such wondrous character and variety. Geomorphological wonders as varied as ocean depths, mountain heights, and vast plains.

But as Paul says in Rom 8:18, all that glory does not even begin to compare with the glory of the age to come, an age of new heavens and a new earth, when creation has been set free from the bondage of corruption. And that is because in the age to come Zion and the new earth will be one. The *whole earth* will be "Jerusalem," filled with glory of the Lord, Num 14:21, as the waters cover the sea, Hab 2:14. The whole earth will be His sanctuary.

This – from Psalm 96 – is just a glimpse of the glory we will enjoy when the Lord returns to Zion:

> *Oh sing to the Lord a new song;*
> *sing to the Lord,* **all the earth**!
> *Sing to the Lord, bless his name;*
> *tell of his salvation from day to day.*
>
> **Declare his glory** *among the nations*
> **his marvelous works** *among all the peoples!*
> *For great is the Lord, and greatly to be praised;*
> *splendor and majesty are before him;*
> *strength and beauty are* **in his sanctuary.**
> *Ascribe to the Lord, O families of the peoples,*
> *ascribe to the Lord glory and strength!*
> *Ascribe to the Lord the glory due his name;*
> *bring an offering, and* **come into his courts**!
> *Worship the Lord in the splendor of holiness;*
> *tremble before him,* **all the earth**!
>
> *Say among the nations, "***The Lord reigns!**
> *Yes,* **the world is established; it shall never be moved;**
> **he will judge the peoples with equity.**"
> *Let the heavens be glad, and* **let the earth rejoice**;
> **let the sea roar,** *and all that fills it;*

> **let the field exult,** *and everything in it!*
> *Then shall **all the trees of the forest sing for joy***
>   *before the* L*ORD**, for he comes,***
> *for **he comes to judge the earth.***
>
> **He will judge the world in righteousness,**
> **and the peoples in his faithfulness.**

Not even Heaven can compare to the glory we will enjoy in Zion, because it will be the best of *both* worlds. Like Heaven, the L*ORD* will be there. Like the earth of Genesis 1, it will be a place created *especially* for us, but now where *all things* have been made new. It will be very, *very*, good.

> *May my tongue stick to the roof of my mouth*
>
>   *if I do not set Zion above my highest joy,*
>
>   *even higher than Heaven.*
>
> *For the heavens are the* L*ORD's heavens but He*
>
>   *has given earth to the children of man.*

Zion's Story

Abbreviations

Bible Versions

CEB	Common English Bible
CSB	Christian Standard Bible
ESV	English Standard Version
LEB	Lexham English Bible
Mounce	Mounce Reverse Interlinear New Testament
NABRE	New American Bible (Revised Edition)
NASB	New American Standard Bible
NET Bible	New English Translation
NIV	New International Version
NRSV	New Revised Standard Version

Other

BDAG	Danker, Bauer, Arndt and Gingrich
BDB	Brown, Driver, Briggs
LN	Louw-Nida
Mounce's	Mounce's Complete Expository Dictionary of Old & New Testament Words
NIDNTTE	New International Dictionary of New Testament Theology and Exegesis
NIDOTTE	New International Dictionary of Old Testament Theology and Exegesis
TDNT	Theological Dictionary of the New Testament
TWOT	Theological Wordbook of the Old Testament

Bibliography

Brown, Francis, 1849-1916. *The Brown, Driver, Briggs Hebrew and English Lexicon : with an Appendix Containing the Biblical Aramaic : Coded with the Numbering System from Strong's Exhaustive Concordance of the Bible* (BDB). Peabody, MA: Hendrickson Publishers, 1996.

Danker, Frederick W., Walter Bauer, William F. Arndt, and F. Wilbur Gingrich. *Greek-English Lexicon of the New Testament and Other Early Christian Literature*, 3rd ed. (BDAG). Chicago: University of Chicago Press, 2000.

Gesenius, Wilhelm. *Hebrew and Chaldee Lexicon to the Old Testament Scriptures*. Translated by Samuel Prideaux Tregelles. London: Samuel Bagster and Sons, 1873.

Harris, R. Laird, Gleason L. Archer Jr., and Bruce K. Waltke, eds. *Theological Wordbook of the Old Testament* (TWOT), 2 vols. Chicago: Moody Press, 1980.

Kittel, Gerhard, G. W. Bromiley, Gerhard Friedrich, and Ronald E. Pitkin. *Theological dictionary of the New Testament* (TDNT), 10 vols. Grand Rapids: Eerdmans, 1964.

Louw, J. P., and E. A. Nida. *Greek-English Lexicon of the New Testament, Based on Semantic Domain* (LN), 2nd ed., 2 vols. New York: United Bible Societies, 1989.

Mounce, William D. *Mounce's Complete Expository Dictionary of Old and New Testament Words*. Grand Rapids: Zondervan, 2006.

Silva, M., ed. *New International Dictionary of New Testament Theology and Exegesis* (NIDNTTE), 2nd ed. 5 vols. Grand Rapids: Zondervan, 2014.

Thayer, Joseph Henry. *The New Thayer's Greek-English Lexicon of the New Testament, With Index*. Peabody, MA: Hendrickson, 1979, 1981.

VanGemeren, Willem A., ed. *New International Dictionary of Old Testament Theology and Exegesis* (NIDOTTE), 5 vols. Grand Rapids: Zondervan, 1997.

Scripture Index

Genesis
1 *50, 64, 120, 123*
1:1 *5 46, 51, 100, 117n76*
1:1, 31a *iii*
1:9 *30*
1:14 *53*
1:26-28 *64, 120*
1:28 *102*
2 *27*
2:1 *46, 51, 100, 117n76*
2:11-14 *27*
3 *27*
3:8 *4, 20-21, 21n14*
10 *28n18, 30*
11:1-9 *28, 28n18*
12:6-9 *41*
13:14-17 *41*
15 *3*
15:18-19 *41*
17:8 *41*
18:17-19 *108*
26:3-5 *41*
28:4, 13-15 *41*
35:2 *49n41*

Exodus
3:1 *2*
4:27 *2*
15:1-18 *1-2*
15:13-18 *48n39*
15:16-18 *1-2*
20-23 *107*
48:8 *47n38*
23:20-33 *108*
24:13 *2*
25:8 *20*

Leviticus
26:11 *22*
26:11-12 *20-21*

Numbers
14:21 *4n4, 64, 122*
21:33-35 *4*
34:2-12 *108*

Deuteronomy
10:14 *33*
12 *3*
12:5-7 *2*
12:5, 11 *4*
14:23 *4*
16:2, 6, 11 *4*
23:14 *21*
30 *58*
30:1-10 *57-60, 59n51*
30:3 *64, 118*
30:5, 6 *59n51*
30:9 *46n36*

Joshua
2:8-11 *2*
11:23 *107*
18:1 *4n4*
21:43-45 *107-108*
23:14 *107-108*

1 Samuel
1:3 *4n4*
2:8 *45n34*

2 Samuel
6:12-15 *1*
7:12-15 *59n51*
7:12-17 *51*

1 Kings
6:1 *1n1*
8:1-11 *2*
8:16, 29 *4n4*
9:3 *4n4*

1 Chronicles
11:4-9 *1*
28:2 *16*

Ezra
9:8-9 *42*

Nehemiah
9:6 *33, 100*
9:36-37 *42*

Job
9:5-7 *49*

Psalms
1, 2 *42*
2:2, 6-8 *42-43*
2:6 *7*
2:6-7 *71n56*
3:4 *7*
8:1-9 *119-120*
11:4 *14, 32*
15:1 *7*
16:10 *39n29*
19:1 *101*
33:6 *100*
37 *41, 55, 67n54*
37:1-11, 18-20, 22, 27-29, 34 *39-41*
37:9, 11, 22, 29, 34 *40n30*
37:18 *43n32*
37:26-27 *53n46*
43:3 *7*
46:4 *82n64*
46:4-5 *9*
46 *12*
47:1-2, 7 *44*
48:1 *25n16*
48:1-3 *2*
51:18 *5n6*
53:6 *118*
66:4 *101*
68 *35, 37n28*
68:7-8, 15-17, 24, 29, 35 *3-4*
68:15-16 *6*

68:16 *31, 35, 46, 48*
68:29, 31 *35-36*
69:34 *101*
72:19 *4n4, 64*
74:2 *1n2*
75:2-3 *49*
75:3 *49, 56, 100*
78:69 *47-48, 47n38*
78:53-54, 60, 67-68 *48*
87:1-2 *2*
87:1-3 *iii*
89 *51*
89:1-37 *52*
89:5 *101*
89:11 *45n34*
89:24-29, 34-37 *52-53*
89:26-27 *53n46*
89:38-51 *52, 52n44*
92:8 *33*
93:1 *45n34*
93:4 *33*
96 *122*
96:7-13 *44-45*
96:10 *45n34, 46, 50*
96:11-12 *101*
97:1, 6 *101*
99:2 *44*
99:5 *16*
99:9 *2, 25n16*
102:19 *32*

102:21 *5n6*
102:25-26 *49*
102:26 *49n41*
103:19 *14*
104:5 *47-50, 47n38, 56, 100*
104:24-25 *101*
110:1 *39n29*
113:4 *33*
113:5 *33*
115:16 *64, 112, 120*
119:89-91 *50-51*
125 *38*
125:1-2 *31, 35, 46, 48*
128:5 *5n6*
132 *38*
132:7 *16*
132:13-14 *93*
132:13-17 *31-32, 35, 46, 48, 70-71*
135:21 *5n6*
137:1-6 *i*
147:2 *5n6*
148:1-5a, 7-13 *101-102*
148:5-6 *47, 51*
148:6 *47n38*

Ecclesiastes
1:4 *47, 47n38*

Isaiah
1:25-27 *6*
2:2-3 *25n16*

4:3-4 *5n6*
7:14 *59n51*
10:12 *5n6*
11:6-9 *46n36, 55n48*
11:9 *4n4, 25n16, 64*
11:11-12 *60, 62*
11:12 *104*
12:3-6 *9, 12*
13:13 *49*
24:23 *5n6*
27:3 *23n16*
30:19 *5n6*
30:29 *25n16*
33:21 *82n64*
34:4 *49*
35:10 *60, 62*
40:1-11 *59n51*
42:5 *100*
43:20-21 *101*
44:24 *100*
45:8, 12, 18 *100*
45:14 *36-37*
45:18 *112*
49:8 *87*
51:6 *49*
51:11 *62*
51:16 *5*
52:1-2 *5n6*
52:7-9 *72-73*
56:6-8 *60-62*

59:18-21 *73*
60:1 *74n58*
60:1-3 *74*
60:10-14 *74-75*
60:11 *75*
60:13 *16, 113-114, 114n74*
60:14 *6*
60:19-20 *82n63*
62:11-12 *6-7*
65, 66 *62n53*
65:11, 25 *25n16*
65:17 *23, 31, 46n36, 62n53, 94*
66:1 *15*
66:1-2a *13-14*
66:15, 24 *62n53*
66:18-20 *61-62*
66:23b *62n53*
66:20 *25n16*
66:22 *23, 31, 46n36, 62n53, 94*

Ezekiel
5:5 *29*
10-11 *71*
11:17, 19-20 *64-65*
11:19 *59n51, 60*
20:40 *25n16*
28 *30*
28:11-16 *26-27*
28:25-26 *65*

28:26 *46n36*
34-37 *79-81*
34:11-16, 25-28 *81*
34:13-14 *46n36, 79*
34:13-14, 25-26, 29-31 *65-66, 79*
34:28-29 *46n36*
36:24, 28, 33-36 *105-106*
36:26-27 *59n51, 60*
37:15-19 *17*
37:15-28 *17, 19, 59n51, 104*
37:20-22, 25-26 *106*
37:20-23 *18*
37:21-22 *66, 79*
37:24-28 *19, 59n51, 110*
37:26-28 *21, 111*
37:26b *109-110*
37:27 *22*
38-39 *29n19, 79-81, 90*
38:7-9 *80*
38:14-16 *80*
38:12 *29, 29n20*
39:7b *80*
39:17 *81*
39:25, 29 *118*
39:25, 28-29 *66*
39:25-29 *81*
40-47 *79*
40:2 *15n11*
43 *12*

43:7a *13, 16, 113-114*
43:7a, 9 *9-10, 93, 110-111*
43:7 *46, 75*
43:7, 9 *32, 35, 38, 46, 48, 71, 114n74*
47 *13*
47:1 *82n64*
47:12 *13*

Jeremiah
3:12-18 *16-17*
3:17 *14, 113-114*
3:18 *17, 104*
7:12 *4n4*
23:3-4 *62*
23:6 *85*
29:10-14 *59n51*
29:14 *62-64, 118*
30-33 *55n48*
30:2-3 *55n48*
30:3 *118*
31:8a, 10-12 *63*
31:23 *7, 118*
31:27, 31, 38 *55n48*
31:31-34 *54*
31:31-36 *54n48*
31:33 *60*
31:35-36 *54*
32:37 *85*
32:37-41 *63*
32:39-40 *60*

33:14 *55n48*
33:16 *85*
33:19-26 *55n48*
Lamentations
2:1 *16*
Daniel
9 *59n51*
9:2-3 *41*
9:16, 20 *7*
Hosea
1:10 *18, 104*
1:11 *104*
2:18 *55n48*
2:23 *18-19, 104*
6:11 *119*
11:9 *10*
Amos
1:2 *5n6*
9:11, 14-15 *105*
9:13-15 *68*
Obadiah
1:20-21 *104*
Micah
2:12 *104-105*
4:1-2 *25n16*
4:2 *5n6*
4:6-7 *68-69*
6:2 *50*
Joel
2 *12*

2:1 *25n16*
2:23, 26-27 *10*
2:28-29 *12*
2:28-32 *83-84*
2:32 *5n6, 71n56, 84*
3 *82*
3:1 *119*
3:1-2, 11-12, 15-17, 20-21 *82-83*
3:16-17 *5n6*
3:17 *25n16*
3:18 *82n64*
Habakkuk
2:14 *4n4, 64, 122*
Zephaniah
3:9-10, 14-17, 20 *36-37*
3:14, 16 *5n6*
3:15-17 *10-11*
3:18-20 *69*
Haggai
2:6-9 *42*
2:6, 21-22 *49*
Zechariah
1:14, 17 *5n6*
2:10-12 *75-76*
2:5, 10-11 *11*
8:3 *25n16*
8:3, 7-8 *11, 76-77*
8:3, 8 *5n6*
8:20-23 *76-77*

8:7-8 *69*
9-14 *82*
9:9-10 *43*
10:6 *104*
10:6-12 *82*
10:8-10 *69*
12:9 *82*
14:1-3 *82*
14:5b-9 *82*
14:9 *45*
Malachi
3:17 *1n2*
Matthew
5:5 *67*
21:15 *43*
24 *87*
24:7-14 *88*
Luke
2:25-32 *59n51*
2:25-32, 36-38 *42*
John
1:3 *116-117, 117n76*
4:20-21 *4n4*
4:21-24 *4n4*
6:38 *14n11*
12:15 *43*
Acts
2 *12, 83*
2:17 *73, 84, 88*
2:17-39 *71n56*

2:28-32 *83-84*
3:19-21 *38, 55*
3:21 *70, 116-117*
13:33 *71n56*
17:11 *94*
Romans
2:29 *19*
4:13 *67*
5:1-5 *102*
8:12-13 *85*
8:18 *122*
8:18-25 *45n35, 102-103*
9:6-8 *18*
9:25-26 *18, 114n74*
10:15 *73*
12:2 *115*
1 Corinthians
10:13b *85*
2 Corinthians
1:19-20 *108-109*
1:20 *70, 74*
3:3 *60*
4:16 *115*
6:1-2 *86*
6:2 *87*
6:16b *86*
Galatians
3:29 *18*
4:28 *18*
6:16 *19*

Ephesians
1:3, 20 *116-117*
1:10 *115-116*
1:13-14 *85*
2:6 *116*
2:22 *86*
3:10 *116*
4:23 *115*
5:14 *74n58*
5:25-33 *114n74*
6:12 *87, 116*
Philippians
3:3 *19*
Colossians
1:16, 20 *115-117*
3:10 *115*
1 Thessalonians
5:2-3 *90*
2 Thessalonians
1:7-8 *90*
2:8 *90*
2 Timothy
3:1 *88*
4:18 *31n22*
Titus
2:11-13 *87*
3:5 *115*
Hebrews
1:2 *88*
1:5 *71n56*
2:5 *112*
2:5-10 *120-121*
5:5 *71n56*
6:4 *31n22*
8:8-12 *54*
9:24 *32*
11:16 *31n22*
12:22 *31n22*
12:22-23 *31n22*
12:22-24 *71n56, 73, 88*
13:4 *114n74*
1 Peter
1:5, 20 *88*
1:8-12 *86-87*
1:10-12 *39n29*
2:9 *1n2, 32n23*
2:10 *19, 114n74*
2 Peter
3 *96*
3:3 *88*
3:7 *100*
3:10-12 *96-100, 97-98n67, 99n69*
3:13 *16n12, 23, 31, 62n53, 73, 94, 115n74*
James
1:10 *99n68*
1 John
2:18 *88*
3:24 *86*

Jude
1:18 *88*

Revelation
1:6 *32n23*
2:26-27 *89*
3:12 *31n22, 71n56*
3:21 *89*
4:11 *100*
5:10 *32n23*
5:13 *101*
6-19 *89*
6:17 *89*
7:13-17 *89*
11:19 *32*
14:1-5 *71n56*
14:3-5 *89*
14:13 *89n66*
19:17-21 *81n62*
20 *89*
20:4-6 *89-90*
20:4-6 *89n66*
20:6 *32n23*
20:7-10 *90*
21 *15*
21-22 *4n4, 12, 14, 14n11 25, 64, 75, 77, 89*
21:1 *16n12, 23, 31, 62n53, 94, 113*
21:1-3 *22, 111, 113*
21:1-5a *95-96*
21:1-5 *116, 117n76*
21:2 *14n11*
21:2, 10 *31n22, 71n56*
21:2-3 *23*
21:3 *21-22*
21:5 *22, 117, 117n76*
21:5a *113*, 115
21:10 *14n11*
21:10-11 *4n4*
21:11, 23 *102n70*
21:23, 25 *82n63*
21:25-26 *75*
22 *13, 46n37*
22:1 *82n64*
22:1-3 *114*
22:1, 3-5 *4n4*
22:1-5 *15*
22:2 *13*
22:5 *82n63*

Made in the USA
Columbia, SC
15 September 2023